mustsees
Chicago

Rookery Building © peterspiro/iStockphoto.com

MICHELIN

mustsees **Chicago**

Editorial Manager	Jonathan P. Gilbert
Contributing Writer	Vince Michael
Production Manager	Natasha G. George
Cartography	Peter Wrenn
Photo Editor	Yoshimi Kanazawa
Photo Research	Nicole D. Jordan
Proofreaders	Liz Jones
Layout	Michelin Apa Publications Ltd.
Interior Design	Chris Bell, cbdesign
Cover Design	Chris Bell, cbdesign, Natasha G. George

Contact Us:

Michelin Travel and Lifestyle
One Parkway South
Greenville, SC 29615
USA
www.michelintravel.com
michelin.guides@us.michelin.com

Michelin TravelPartner
Hannay House
39 Clarendon Road
Watford, Herts WD17 1JA
UK
(01923) 205 240
www.ViaMichelin.com
travelpubsales@uk.michelin.com

Special Sales:

For information regarding bulk sales, customized
editions, and premium sales, please contact
our Customer Service Departments:

USA	1-800-432-6277
UK	(01923) 205 240
Canada	1-800-361-8236

Michelin Apa Publications Ltd
58 Borough High Street, London SE1 1XF, United Kingdom

Note to the reader:
While every effort is made to ensure that all information printed in this guide is correct and
up to date, Michelin Apa Publications Ltd. accepts no liability for any direct, indirect, or
consequential losses howsoever caused so far as such can be excluded by law. Admission
prices listed for sights in this guide are for a single adult, unless otherwise specified.

View of Gold Coast on the Lake Michigan in the evening

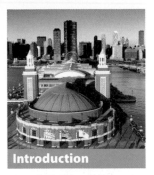

Introduction

City of Big Shoulders:
Chicago, Illinois 20

Must Sees

TABLE OF CONTENTS

★★★ ATTRACTIONS

Unmissable attractions awarded three stars in this guide include:

The Field Museum p 46

© Greg Neise/The Field Museum

Willis (Sears) Tower p 39

©reb/Fotolia.com

Cloud Gate in
Millennium Park p 62

©Mario Savoia/Bigstockphoto.com/

Auditorium Building p 22

©James Caulfield, from *Louis Sullivan: Creating a New American*

MUST KNOW

Jay Pritzker Pavilion p 61

John Hancock Center p 38

Oak Park p 78

Museum of Science and Industry p 48

Art Institute of Chicago p 44

STAR ATTRACTIONS

★★★ ATTRACTIONS

Unmissable sights in Chicago

For more than 75 years people have used the Michelin stars to take the guesswork out of travel. Our star-rating system helps you make the best decision on where to go, what to do, and what to see.

★★★	Unmissable
★★	Worth a trip
★	Worth a detour
No star	Recommended

★★★Three-Stars

★★Two-Stars

★One-Star

MUST KNOW

ACTIVITIES

Unmissable activities, entertainment, restaurants and hotels

We recommend every activity in this guide, but the Michelin Man highlights our top picks.

Culture

Intuit: The Center for Intuitive
    and Outsider Art *p 56*
National American Italian Sports
    Hall of Fame *p 58*

Kids

ComedySportz4Kids *p 101*
American Girl Place *p 100*
Children's Museum
    of Immigration *p 101*

Nightlife

Double Door *p 115*
New Checkerboard Lounge
    for Blues 'n' Jazz *p 115*
The Second City *p 118*
The Violet Hour *p 117*
Zanies *p 118*

Recreation

Ice skating at Daley
    Bicentennial Plaza *p 92*
High Tea at the Drake Hote *p 30*

Restaurants

avec *p 130*
Custom House *p 127*
Green Zebra *p 127*
L20 *p 125*
Pizzeria Due *p 101*
Pizzeria Uno *p 101*

Shops

Armitage Avenue *p 104*
Leslie Hindman Auctioneers *p 108*
Southport Avenue *p 104*
The 900 Shops *p 103*

Spas

Asha *p 110*
Kiva Day Spa *p 111*

Theater

Biograph Theater at Victory
    Gardens Theater *p 90, p 123*
Steppenwolf Theatre *p 123*

Tours

Architecture Foundation Tours *p 32*
Chicago River Tours *p 42*
Untouchable Tours *p 89*

CALENDAR OF EVENTS

Listed below is a selection of Chicago's most popular annual events. Please note that dates may change from year to year.

For more detailed information, contact the Chicago Office of Tourism: 312-744-2400 or www.cityofchicago.org.

February

Chinese New Year Parade
Wentworth Ave. from
Cermak Rd. to 24th St.
312-744-3315
www.cityofchicago.org/
specialevents

March

Chicago Flower and Garden Show
Navy Pier
312-595-PIER
www.chicagoflower.com

St. Patrick's Day Parade
Columbus Dr., from Balbo Ave.
to Monroe St.
312-744-3315

April

Major League Baseball Opening Day
Chicago Cubs
Wrigley Field
773-404-2827
http://chicago.cubs.mlb.com
Chicago White Sox
U.S. Cellular Field
312-674-1000
www.chisox.com

May

ArtChicago
Merchandise Mart,
222 Merchandise Mart Plaza
800-677-6262
www.artchicago.com

Chicago Summer Neighborhood Festivals
Various locations (May–Sept)
312-744-3315

www.cityofchicago.org/
specialevents

International Antiques Fair
Merchandise Mart,
222 Merchandise Mart Plaza
800-677-6278
www.merchandisemart.com/
chicagoantiques

Kids and Kites Festival
Montrose Beach, Lincoln Park
312-744-3315
www.cityofchicago.org/
specialevents

June

Chicago Blues Festival
Grant Park
312-744-3315
www.cityofchicago.org/
specialevents

Chicago Gospel Festival
Millennium Park
312-744-3315
www.chicagogospelmusic
festival.us

Old Town Art Fair
1763 N. North Park Ave.
312-337-1938
www.oldtownartfair.org

57th Street Art Fair
1507 E. 53rd St.
773-493-3247
www.57thstreetartfair.org

Ravinia Festival
Highland Park (Jun–Sept)
847-266-5100
www.ravinia.org

Taste of Chicago
Grant Park
312-744-3315
www.tasteofchicago.us

MUST KNOW

July

Grant Park Music Festival
Grant Park
312-742-7638
www.grantparkmusic
festival.com

Pitchfork Music Festival
Union Park
www.pitchforkmusic
festival.com

August

Bud Billiken Day Parade
King Dr. between 35th St. and
55th St.
312-536-3710
www.budbillikenparade.com

Chicago Air & Water Show
North Avenue Beach
312-744-3315
www.chicagoairand
watershow.us

Lollapalooza
Grant Park
www.lollapalooza.com

September

Chicago Jazz Festival
Petrillo Bandshell, Grant Park
312-744-3315
www.chicagojazzfestival.us

World Music Festival
Various locations
312-742-1938
www.cityofchicago.org/
worldmusic

October

**Chicago International
Film Festival**
Various theaters
312-683-0121
www.chicagofilmfestival.com

Chicago Marathon
Ends at Grant Park
312-904-9800
www.chicagomarathon.com

November

Day of the Dead Celebration
National Museum of Mexican
Art, 1852 W. 19th St.
312-738-1503
www.nationalmuseumof
mexicanart.org

Mag Mile Lights Festival
N. Michigan Ave.
312-642-3570
www.themagnificentmile.com

December

Winter Wonder Fest
Navy Pier (www.navypier.com)
312-595-PIER

June Taste of Chicago at Grant Park

© City of Chicago / GRC

CALENDAR OF EVENTS

PRACTICAL INFORMATION

WHEN TO GO

Spring is temperamental, with conditions fluctuating from cold to warm and back again. Although open-air activities are limited, the winter and spring months can be a prime time to make the most of lower hotel rates and indoor treasures.

Summer is the high tourist season, offering countless festivals and opportunities for outdoor recreation—along with hot and humid weather, and, often, rain (June, July, and August are statistically the rainiest months).

Fall is also popular, when crowds thin, the humidity disappears and the temperatures cool. Snow poses little threat until late November, when the infamous Chicago **winter** blows in: You'll be cold, but attractions won't be crowded.

KNOW BEFORE YOU GO

Before you go, consider obtaining maps and information about sightseeing, accommodations, travel packages, recreational opportunities, and seasonal events.

Chicago Convention and Tourism Bureau
2301 S. Lakeshore Dr.,
Chicago, IL 60616
312-567-8500;
www.choosechicago.com

Useful Websites
Here are some additional websites to help you plan your trip:

www.877chicago.com
www.metromix.com
www.themagnificentmile.com
www.chicago.il.org
www.chicagonews.com
www.chicagolandchamber.org
www.choosechicago.com

Chicago Office of Tourism
78 E. Washington St.,
Chicago, IL 60602
312-744-2400;
http://egov.cityofchicago.org

Visitor Information Centers
Chicago Cultural Center
78 E. Randolph St.; *312-744-6630*
Open year-round Mon–Thu 8am–7pm, Fri 8am–6pm, Sat 10am–6pm, Sun 11am–5pm. Closed holidays.

Sears on State Information Kiosk
2 N. State St., at Madison Ave.
Open year-round Mon–Sat 10am–6pm, Sun noon–5pm. Closed Thanksgiving Day & Dec 25.

International Visitors

Visitors from outside the US can obtain information from the Chicago Convention and Tourism Bureau *(312-567-8500 or 877-244-2246; www.choosechicago.com)* or

Average Seasonal Temperatures in Chicago				
	Jan	Apr	July	Oct
Avg. high	29°F/-2°C	58°F/15°C	83°F/28°C	63°F/18°C
Avg. low	13°F/-10°C	38°F/4°C	62°F/17°C	42°F/6°C

MUST KNOW

from the US embassy or consulate in their country of residence. For a complete list of American consulates and embassies abroad, visit the US State Department Bureau of Consular Affairs listing on the internet at: *http://travel. state.gov*.

Entry Requirements

Travelers entering the United States under the Visa Waiver Program (VWP) must have a machine-readable passport. Any traveler without a machine-readable passport will be required to obtain a visa before entering the US. Citizens of VWP countries are permitted to enter the US for general business or tourist purposes for a maximum of 90 days without needing a visa. Requirements for the Visa Waiver Program can be found at the Department of State's Visa Services website *(http://travel.state.gov)*. All citizens of nonparticipating countries must have a visitor's visa. Upon entry, nonresident foreign visitors must present a valid passport and round-trip transportation ticket. Canadian citizens are not required to present a passport or visa, but they must present a valid picture ID and proof of citizenship. Naturalized Canadian citizens should carry their citizenship papers.

US Customs

All articles brought into the US must be declared at the time of entry. Prohibited items include: plant material, firearms and ammunition (if not for sporting purposes), and meat or poultry products. For information, contact the US Customs Service, 1300 Pennsylvania Ave. NW, Washington, DC 20229 *(202-354-1000; www.cbp.gov)*.

GETTING THERE
By Air

Chicago is serviced by two international airports:
O'Hare International Airport (ORD) is one of the world's busiest airports. Located 17 miles northwest of downtown, O'Hare is served by most major carriers *(take I-90 West to Exit 78/I-190 West; 773-686-2200 or 800-832-6352; www.ohare.com)*. **Midway International Airport (MDW)** has more commuter air traffic and is much less crowded than O'Hare. It's located 10 miles southwest of downtown *(take I-90 South to I-55 West to Exit 286/Cicero Ave.; 773-686-2200 or 800-832-6352; www.flychicago.com)*.
Airport Transfers – **Airport Express** offers shuttles between O'Hare, Midway, downtown hotels, and North Shore suburbs year-round. Shuttles run between airports and downtown hotels daily. Agents available 6am–10:30pm; 24 hour reservations can be made on-line *(888-284-3826; www.airport express.com; one passenger/ one-way fare is $23 from O'Hare Airport)*. Tickets are available at Airport Express counters, located across from the baggage-claim areas.
Chicago Transit Authority trains service both airports: the Blue Line runs to the Loop from O'Hare; the Orange Line train services Midway *(for schedule and fare information, see p15)*.
Taxi service from the airports to downtown averages $30 to $35 from O'Hare and $25 to $30 from Midway.

By Train

Amtrak *(800-872-7245 or www.amtrak.com)* runs several lines to Chicago's Union Station, on the Near West Side *(210 S. Canal St.; 312-655-2524)*.

By Bus

Greyhound *(800-229-9424 or www.greyhound.com)* provides bus service to Chicago's main bus terminal, located on the Near West Side *(630 W. Harrison St.; 312-408-5800 or 800-231-2222)*. The new **Megabus** *(800-402-6342 or www.megabus.com)* has low-priced fares to other Midwestern cities. Bus stops vary according to the route.

By Car

Chicago is easily accessible from a number of major highways. The Dan Ryan Expressway (I-90/I-94), the Chicago Skyway (toll road), and I-57 serve the south side, while the Stevenson Expressway (I-55) offers access to the southwest. The Eisenhower Expressway (I-290), called Congress Parkway within downtown, provides the quickest route to the western suburbs. The Kennedy (I-90/94) and Edens (I-94) expressways serve the northwest and north sides respectively. Lake Shore Drive (US-41) follows the lakefront through the city to the northern suburbs. The I-294 (Tri-state Tollway) beltway rings western Chicago.

GETTING AROUND
By Car

The interstates around Chicago tend to be heavily trafficked, no matter the time of day. Parking downtown can be a hassle; in general, you're better off walking or taking public transportation.

If you do have a car, avoid driving during commuter rush hours *(weekdays 7:30am–9am & 4–6pm)*. Use of seat belts is required. Child safety seats are mandatory for children under 7 years of age.

Driving in the US – Visitors bearing valid driver's licenses issued by their country of residence are not required to obtain an International Driver's License. Drivers must carry vehicle registration and/or rental contract, and proof of automobile insurance at all times. Gasoline is sold by the gallon (1 gallon = 3.8 liters). Vehicles in the US are driven on the right-hand side of the road.

Parking – Street parking can be difficult to find and public parking garages are expensive (downtown garage parking averages $7 to $17 for one to four hours). Note that your vehicle will be towed from the street and some parking lots if left overnight.

Many streets are designated Snow Routes (indicated by red, white, and blue signs); parking is not allowed on either side of these streets overnight during winter or when there are two or more inches of snow on the ground.

No parking is allowed on many streets during rush hour and during specific street-cleaning days; check signs before you leave your car. Parking in some residential areas is restricted to area residents.

By Public Transportation

The **Chicago Transit Authority (CTA)** operates an efficient and extensive network of **subways**, elevated trains and trolleys. Schedules and route information are available at most train stations, as well as through the CTA *(888-*

968-7282 or www.transitchicago.com). **Pace Bus** *(847-364-7223; www.pacebus.com)* provides bus service throughout the suburbs. CTA route maps and brochures are available online, as well as at both airports, train stations, and at City of Chicago information booths. Chicago's **Travel Information Hotline** is available seven days a week *(4:45am–1am)* from any Chicago area code: *836-7000*.
Elevated Commuter Rail Line – *See map on inside back cover*. Known to locals as the "El," this elevated train runs through the Loop and connects all cardinal points of the city and suburbs through a system of colored lines such as the Red Line, running north–south; the Green Line, running west–south; the Blue Line, taking a west–northwest route through Wicker Park to O'Hare Airport; the Brown Line, a scenic, above-ground route running north; and the Orange Line, a connection to Midway Airport. Basic fare is $1.75; transfers are an extra 25¢ (for two transfers within two hours of ticket purchase).
Trains operate daily 5am–1am; the Red and Blue lines operate 24 hours a day. **Visitor passes**, which allow unlimited rides on all CTA

Navy Pier Trolley

Want to take the kids to Navy Pier? Sure, you do! But it can be a hike from hotels in the Loop. Never fear. Hop aboard the free trolley that runs daily between the pier and State Street, along Grand Avenue and Illinois Street (trolley stops are marked with signs). Trolleys run about every 20 minutes *(Mon–Thu 10am–9pm, Fri & Sat 10am–11pm, Sun 10am–9pm)*.

buses and trains, are available at train stations and visitor centers, or online *(1 day/$5; 2 days/$9; 3 days/$12; 5 days/$18)*. Purchase a fare card or visitor pass for access to city buses as well. Bus fares are $2 with exact cash, versus $1.75 with a fare card.

By Taxi

Cabs are readily available at all hours; you can hail cabs on the street, or find them outside major hotels. Riders are required to pay the fare shown on the meter, plus any tolls. The meter starts at $1.90 for the first mile, and $1.60 for each additional mile, or $2 for each minute of waiting time. Major cab companies include: **Flash Cab**

Chicago Greeters

First time in Chicago? Take a free tour with one of Chicago's official greeters *(312-744-8000; www.chicagogreeter.com; tours held Mon–Fri 9am–5pm)*. These savvy guides enjoy sharing their knowledge and love of the Windy City. Set aside a morning or afternoon to explore neighborhoods, parks, cultural elements, and, of course, the indispensable shops and restaurants. Tours can be one-on-one or group-oriented; "themed" tours offer jaunts for everyone from the literature buff to the sports enthusiast. Short on time? Try "Insta Greeter," the first-come, first-served free mini-tour; it lets you explore downtown in an hour with a local volunteer greeter.

Car Rental		
Car Rental Company	**Reservations**	**Internet**
Alamo	800-462-5266	www.alamo.com
Avis	800-331-1212	www.avis.com
Budget	800-527-0700	www.budget.com
Dollar	800-800-3665	www.dollar.com
Enterprise	800-261-7331	www.enterprise.com
Hertz	800-654-3131	www.hertz.com
National	800-227-7368	www.nationalcar.com
Thrifty	800-847-4389	www.thrifty.com

(773-561-4444; www.flashcab. com), **Yellow Cab** *(312-829-4222; www.yellowcabchicago.com)*, and **Checker Cab** *(312-243-2537)*.

By Water
From Memorial Day to Labor Day, **Shoreline Sightseeing** *(312-222-9328; www.shorelinesightseeing. com)* operates water taxis on Lake Michigan between Navy Pier and Shedd Aquarium, and along the Chicago River from Navy Pier to the Sears Tower. Fares for a one-way ticket are $6 for adults, and $3 for children under 12. An all-day pass costs $12 for adults, $6 for children under 12.

By Foot
Put on your comfortable shoes. Walking is one of the best ways to explore Chicago, particularly the Loop, River North, and the Magnificent Mile neighborhoods.

ACCESSIBILITY
Disabled Travelers
Federal law requires that businesses (including hotels and restaurants) provide access for the disabled, devices for the hearing impaired, and designated parking spaces. For further information, contact the Society for Accessible Travel and Hospitality **(SATH)** *(347 Fifth Ave., Suite 605, New York, NY 10016; 212-447-7284; www.sath.org)*. All national parks have facilities for the disabled, and offer free or discounted passes.
For details, contact the **National Park Service** *(Office of Public Inquiries, P.O. Box 37127, Room 1013, Washington, DC 20013-7127; 202-208-4747; www.nps.gov)*. Passengers who will need assistance with train or bus travel should give advance notice to **Amtrak** *(800-872-7245 or 800-523-6590/TDD; www.amtrak.com)* or Greyhound *(800-752-4841 or 800-345-3109/TDD; www.greyhound. com)*. Make reservations for hand-controlled cars in advance with the rental company.
Local Lowdown – Additional detailed information about access

for the disabled in the Chicago area is available from the **Mayor's Office for People with Disabilities** *(121 North LaSalle St.; Room 1104, Chicago, IL 60602; 312-744-7050; www.cityofchicago.org)*. They also publish a monthly newsletter called **AccessNotes**, which is available from their office. For information about disabled access to public transportation, contact the **Chicago Transit Authority** *(312-432-7025; www.transitchicago.com)*.

Senior Citizens

Many hotels, attractions, and restaurants offer discounts to visitors aged 62 or older (proof of age may be required). The **AARP**, formerly the American Association of Retired Persons, offers discounts to its members *(601 E St. NW, Washington, DC 20049; 202-424-3410; www.aarp.com)*.

ACCOMMODATIONS

For a list of suggested accommodations, see Must Stay. An area visitors' guide including lodging directory is available free of charge from the Chicago Convention and Tourism Bureau *(see p12)*.

Hotel Reservation Services

At Home Inn Chicago – 312-640-1050 or 800-375-7084. www.at homeinnchicago.com. Focuses on city-style B&B accommodations.
Hot Rooms – *773-468-7666 or 800-468-3500. www.hotrooms.com*.
Hotel Reservations Network – *800-715-7666. www.hoteldiscount.com*.
Hotels.com – 800-346-8357. www.hotels.com.

Illinois Hotel & Lodging Association – *877-456-3446. www.stayillinois.com*.

Hostels

Hostels are a great choice for budget travelers. Prices average $17 to $35 per night for a dorm-style room.
Chicago International Hostel – 6318 N. Winthrop Ave., Lakeview. *773-262-1011. www.hostelworld.com*.
Hostelling International Chicago – 24 E. Congress Pkwy. at Wabash St., in the Loop. *312-360-0300. www.hichicago.org*.

COMMUNICATIONS
Area Codes

To call between different area codes in Chicago, dial 1 + area code + seven-digit number. The same applies to local calls, even within the same area code.
Chicago (downtown)**: 312**
Chicago (other areas)**: 773**
Northern suburbs (Evanston)**: 847**
Southern suburbs (Oak Park)**: 708**
Western suburbs: 630
Outer suburbs: 815

Internet Access

Free wireless internet access is available across Chicago; see www.wififreespot.com to find the nearest WiFi spot to you. There are also plenty of internet cafés around the city; ask at visitor information centers or at your hotel.

Newspapers

Chicago's two main daily morning newspapers are the *Chicago Tribune* and the *Chicago Sun-Times.* For news of what's going on when you're in town, check out the entertainment sections of the

Emergency (Police/Ambulance/Fire Department, 24hrs)	✆**911**
Police (non-emergency, within Chicago)	✆311
Poison Control	✆312-942-5969
Physician Referral	✆312-926-8400
Chicago Medical Society	✆312-670-2550
Dental Emergencies	
Chicago Dental Society	✆312-836-7300
24-hour Pharmacy: Walgreens	
757 N. Michigan Ave., Magnificent Mile	✆312-664-4000
111. S. Halsted St., Near West Side	✆312-463-9139
1601 N. Wells St., Old Town	✆312-642-4738
641 N. Clark St., South Loop	✆312-587-0904
Time	✆312-976-1616
Weather	✆312-976-1212

Tribune (Friday) and the *Sun-Times* (*Weekend Plus* section), both published on Fridays.

Two weekly alternatives (published Thursday) are the *Chicago Reader* and *Time Out Chicago*.

These offer good coverage of the arts and nightlife. A great resource for last-minute dining and nightlife events is *http://312diningdiva.com*.

DISCOUNTS

To find Chicago's many discounted offers, start with a look at *www.explorechicago.org/city*. Some of the main discounted passes to benefit from are:

CityPass – *$76 adults; $59 children ages 3–11; good for nine consecutive days*. This gives you discounted VIP admission to some of the major attractions. You can purchase a CityPass at participating attractions, or at *www.citypass.com*.

Metra 10-Ticket Ride – 15 percent off one-way fares on city rail. *http://metrarail.com*.

$5 Weekend Pass – Unlimited city rail travel at the weekend (not South Shore).

GoChigago Card – *Available for 1, 3, 5, or 7 days, from $66.99 to $169.99 adults; $44.99 to $129.99 children*. An all-access pass to all kinds of attractions, and a free guided tour per day. *www.smartdestinations.com*.

ELECTRICITY

Voltage in the US is 120 volts AC, 60 Hz. Foreign-made appliances may need AC adapters (available at specialty travel and electronics stores) and North American flat-blade plugs.

MONEY AND CURRENCY EXCHANGE

Visitors can exchange currency downtown in the Loop at the following;

◆ **Northern Trust Company** *(50 S. LaSalle St.; 312-630-6000; www.northerntrust.com; Mon–Fri 9am–5pm),*

◆ **Chase Bank** *(10 S. Dearborn and 21 S. Clark St., 312-732-1174).*

◆ **World's Money Exchange, Inc.** *(203 N. LaSalle St., Suite M-11; 312-641-2151; www.wmeinc.com; open Mon–Fri 9am–5pm)*

◆ **American Express Travel Service** *(605 N. Michigan Ave.; 312-943-7840 www.american express.com; open Mon–Fri 8:30am –5:30pm).* **American Express®** also has an office on the Magnificent Mile *(605 N. Michigan Ave., Suite 105; 312-435-2570; open Mon–Fri 8:30am–6pm, Sat 9am–5pm).*

O'Hare International Airport Currency Exchange offices *(773-686-7965)* are located on the lower level of the international terminal, at Arrivals Door A.

For cash transfers, **Western Union** *(800-325-6000; www.western union.com)* has agents throughout Chicago. Banks, stores, restaurants, and hotels accept traveler's checks with photo identification.

To report a lost or stolen credit card: **American Express®** *(800-528-4800)*; **Diners Club®** *(800-234-6377)*; **MasterCard®** *(800-307-7309)*; **Visa®** *(800-336-8472)*.

OPENING HOURS
Visiting Attractions
Most attractions open their doors at 9am and close them at 5pm. Be sure to check before visiting.

Shopping
Stores tend to open Mon–Sat 10am–6 or 7pm, Sun noon–6pm.

SMOKING
Despite a number of opposers, Chicago followed other cities around the world by imposing a smoking ban in 2008. Public places, including restaurants, clubs, and theaters, are all smoke free.

SPECTATOR SPORTS
Sports are as essential a part of Chicago as the wind, the lake and deep-dish pizza, so if you like sports, attending a game should be on your "to do" list. Availability of tickets is in direct proportion to how well the team in question is doing. If the Bears are Super Bowl-bound, you won't find a ticket at all, and even when they aren't, **American football** tickets can be expensive bought from a ticket broker. **Basketball** (the Bulls) and **baseball** (the Cubs and the White Sox) are generally available during the regular season. Since Americans haven't embraced hockey and soccer as fervently, Blackhawks and Fire tickets are easier to find. No matter what team you see, you're sure to encounter enthusiastic fans and a quintessential Chicago experience.

TAXES AND TIPPING
Prices displayed in Chicago do not include sales tax of 10.25 percent, which is not reimbursable. It is customary to give a gift of money—a tip—for services rendered, to waiters (15–20 percent of bill), porters ($1 per bag), chambermaids ($1 per day), and cab drivers (15 percent of fare).

TIME ZONE
Chicago is in the **Central Time** (CT) zone, one hour behind New York City and six hours behind Greenwich Mean Time.

CHICAGO, ILLINOIS

Chicago (population close to 3 million) was never destined to be a great city; the odds, from the get-go, were stacked against it. But mud, fire, labor unrest, gangsters, shady politics, and the Cubs only seem to have strengthened Chicago's character. Settled in 1779 by Jean-Baptiste Point du Sable on a swampy riverbank, Chicago takes its name from the native Potawatomi word She-caw-gu, meaning "stinking onion"—a reference to the garlic that grew wild in the area.

Chicago Grows Up – At first glance, it is hard to understand how and why Chicago turned from a mere town of 4,000 in 1837, when the city was incorporated, to 300,000 people by 1871 and 1.5 million at the turn of the 20C. The quagmire on which the city was built thwarted construction and contributed to the spread of disease. In the 1850s, Chicago stank. Much-needed sewer lines were placed at street level and

Carl Sandburg's Chicago

"Hog Butcher for the World,
Tool Maker, Stacker of Wheat,
Player with Railroads and the
Nation's Freight Handler:
Stormy, husky, brawling,
City of the Big Shoulders . . ."

Carl Sandburg, 1916, *Chicago*

the streets and structures raised around them. To stem overflow and sewage dumped into the Chicago River, and to protect drinking water and prevent cholera, a scheme was hatched to reverse the river's flow away from the lake. By 1900 engineers finally succeeded in permanently reversing the river's flow. Despite those setbacks, Chicago's location between the Mississippi River and the Great Lakes became a strategic advantage for a growing America. Lumber, grain, and livestock funneled through Chicago in extraordinary quantities. Tunnels, bridges, and roads were built to accommodate the busy metropolis, and immigrants arrived in droves to do the work.

In October 1871, the **Great Chicago Fire** broke out, burning

Engraving of *The Burning of Chicago* (c. 1883) by R. H. Stoddard

Chicago skyline and Navy Pier

© City of Chicago / GRC

for three days and destroying the central city. Stubborn and proud locals began rebuilding immediately and growth continued unabated; the population tripled in the decade following the fire. In spite of crowding, poor sanitation and grueling working conditions, Chicago rose above the murk of its stockyards and steel mills. After 1880, the central city grew tall on the talents of a coterie of architects who pioneered the Chicago School of Architecture.

By the 1890s, elite residents had leisure time and money enough to establish cultural institutions. The crowning achievement would be the staging of the **World's Columbian Exposition** (see p67) in 1893 on the South Side lakefront. A showcase of Neoclassical architecture and modern technology, the fair established Chicago as a world-class city.

Bootleggers and Power Brokers – The Roaring Twenties left a permanent mark, as bootlegging gangsters, the best-known being **Al Capone**, murdered many in attempts to control the illegal liquor business. Another power broker came into his own

when the Democratic Machine hit its stride under Richard J. Daley in 1955. His "City that Works" did so because the mayor knew how to exchange influence to get things done. Daley died in 1976. When Harold Washington, the city's first black mayor, triumphantly took office in 1983, many looked forward to a new chapter. However, Washington died unexpectedly in office four years later. Waiting in the wings, Richard M. Daley rose to assume his father's throne for nearly 22 years, greatly beautifying the city. Rahm Emanuel now leads complex Chicago into the 21C.

Chicago Fast Facts and Firsts

- Chicago covers **228 square miles**.
- The city is home to **2.8 million people**.
- Chicago **invented** the zipper, Twinkies, and the smoke-filled room.
- Chicago birthed the **first skyscraper** and the first controlled atomic reaction.
- In 2007 alone, 91 **movies** and TV shows were filmed in Chicago.
- The **Chicago Board of Trade** is the world's oldest and largest futures exchange.

21

NEIGHBORHOODS

Chicago is a city of neighborhoods—urban, busy, sometimes crowded, yes, but also tree-lined and intimate. From the Far South Side, up through Bronzeville and Chinatown, around Pilsen, and then through the Loop into the upscale neighborhoods of the Magnificent Mile and the Gold Coast, to the North Side's vibrancy, the patchwork that is Chicago offers something new, literally, around each corner.

THE LOOP★★★

See map on inside front cover.

Looming large along the lakefront, south of the Chicago River, the city's busy Loop has been fertile ground for architectural innovation since the fire in 1871 destroyed the downtown business district. Named for the elevated tracks that circle them, these blocks bustle with workday energy as Chicagoans transact their daily business in office towers that catalog the city's skyward growth since the 19C. State Street★ has renewed its traditional role as a busy shopping corridor (see pp26, 103), and in the evenings, the Loop offers a selection of theater, music, and dining experiences.

IN THE LOOP

Auditorium Building★★★

Auditorium Building

©Chicago Architecture Foundation/Anne Evans

50 E. Congress Pkwy. 312-431-2360. www.auditoriumtheatre.org. Tours Mon 10:30am and noon, Thu 10:30am. $10 per person. Groups scheduled at 312-4531-2389 ext. 0.

This cornerstone of the Loop's east side launched the careers of architects Louis Sullivan and Dankmar Adler, as well as a young draftsman named Frank Lloyd Wright (see p79). Completed in 1889, it housed a hotel, an office

---

Looping the Loop

Most Chicagoans agree that the best way to explore the Loop is on foot. However, the city offers some fun alternative methods of getting around this neighborhood:

- ◆ **By Boat** – The best way to see Chicago's skyscrapers is from the river. Cruises depart from the docks on both sides of the Michigan Avenue Bridge, near the **Riverwalk★**, a great place for a stroll in nice weather. *For more information on river tours, see p42.*
- ◆ **By the "L"** – Take the elevated Brown Line (Ravenswood) to circle the Loop.
- ◆ **By Train** – A free 40-minute train tour affords the same views as the "L" *(offered on a first-come, first-served basis May–Sept, Sat 11:35am & 12:55pm)*.

Public Sculpture in the Loop

Chicago Stock Exchange Arch
* Dankmar Adler and Louis Sullivan
Art Institute, Columbus Dr. entrance

Monument with Standing Beast
* Jean Dubuffet
James R. Thompson Center Plaza

The Seated Lincoln
* Augustus Saint-Gaudens
Grant Park, Court of Presidents

Untitled
* Pablo Picasso *Daley Center Plaza*

Flamingo
* Alexander Calder
Federal Center Plaza

Four Seasons
* Marc Chagall
First National Bank Plaza

Miró's Chicago
* Joan Miró
Washington St., next to Chicago Temple

tower, and a theater and was Chicago's tallest building at the time. The spectacular theater remains an acoustic marvel; enter the lobby on Congress Parkway to see some of Sullivan's intricate designs. Better yet, reserve tickets for one of the dance or musical theater productions held here between November and June.

Former Location of Carson Pirie Scott & Company★★★

1 S. State St.

Architect Louis Sullivan's incredible skill with ornament is evident in the cast iron that embroiders the building's rounded front corner. Indeed, this 1899 structure represents the height of Sullivan's ornamental genius.

It was once one of State Street's duo of historic department stores. Development is under way to convert the space into a gourmet grocery, restaurant, and retail and office space.

Chicago Cultural Center★★

78 E. Washington St. 312-744-6630. http://egov.cityofchicago.org. Open year-round Mon–Thu 8am–7pm, Fri 8am–6pm, Sat 9am–6pm, Sun 10am–6pm. Closed major holidays.

Former Carson Pirie Scott & Company Building

©Vince Michael/Michelin

NEIGHBORHOODS

Chicago Cultural Center

City of Chicago/Hedrick Blessing

This marvelous Neoclassical palace was the city's first library when it was completed in 1897. Today it functions as an all-purpose exhibition, arts, and music center, and also houses the **Chicago Office of Tourism Visitor Information Center** *(312-744-2400)*. Enter from Washington Street and ascend the grand staircase to **Preston-Bradley Hall★** (note the restored Tiffany stained-glass dome), where free concerts are offered Monday through Friday at 12:15pm and on Sunday at 3pm.

Touring Tip

For a good panorama of the north side of the river, venture to the corner of Clark Street and Wacker Drive. That massive pile to the left is the **Merchandise Mart**, all 4.1 milion square feet of it (see box, p106) . To the right, the corncob towers of Marina City stand out, and just east of them, the IBM Building. Below it, the Sun-Times headquarters and printing press once stood; it was demolished in 2004 to make way for the new Trump Tower, scheduled for completion in 2009.

Chicago School of Architecture

Fortunately, without a time machine you can get a glimpse of what 19C Chicago looked like while you're in the Loop. For a sense of scale, head to the 16-story **Monadnock Building★★** *(53 W. Jackson Blvd.)*, the tallest masonry structure in Chicago; the **Marquette Building★★** *(140 S. Dearborn St.)*, whose lobby features a stunning **Tiffany glass mosaic** illustrating the journeys of French explorer Jacques Marquette; and the **Rookery★★** *(southeast corner of LaSalle & Adams Sts.)*, which some think was named for the pigeons who invaded a temporary city hall built here in 1871. The lobby was designed in 1905 by Frank Lloyd Wright. Once your eye becomes familiar with the style, you'll spot many others.

Federal Center★★

On Dearborn St., between Adams St. & Jackson Blvd.

Completed in 1974, this three-building complex is a wonderful example of the steel-and-glass International style for which architect Ludwig Mies van der Rohe became so famous. Seemingly unadorned, its beauty depends on its perfect proportions. The restrained buildings form a perfect frame for Alexander Calder's fiery, flamboyant sculpture **Flamingo** (1973).

James R. Thompson Center★★

100 Randall St. Bounded by Clark, LaSalle, Randolph & Lake Sts.

Architectural "bad boy" Helmut Jahn, known for bucking accepted

Scraping the Sky

A talented and energetic group of architects—William Le Baron Jenney, Louis Sullivan, William Holabird, Martin Roche, Daniel Burnham, John Wellborn Root, and others—rebuilt Chicago after the 1871 fire. Within a year, 10,000 new buildings rose up at a cost of $45 million. By 1890 the booming population needed more offices. With no place to go but up, Chicago architects and engineers created the skyscraper. In traditional masonry construction, thick walls support the weight of the building, but architect William Le Baron Jenney (1832–1907) reversed the formula by hanging "curtain" walls on a skeletal steel frame, allowing buildings to grow taller. Based on this steel-frame construction, Jenney's 1884 now demolished, nine-story Home Insurance Building is considered the first modern skyscraper. Engineers mastered ways to anchor tall buildings in Chicago's swampy soil and to reduce the effects of high winds. Improvements to the elevator and the telephone made vertical height practical. Thus, the **Chicago School of Architecture** was born, recognized as the first significant new movement in architecture since the Italian High Renaissance.

trends, designed this State of Illinois facility to resemble the domes you're used to seeing on government buildings. Though quirky, the shape makes possible the soaring **atrium**, which rises the full 17 stories and encloses open office floors. Catch a snack at the lower-level food court and enjoy the constantly changing play of light and shadow that filters into the airy space. **Monument with Standing Beast**, a curvaceous fiberglass sculpture by Jean Dubuffet, adorns the plaza.

Richard J. Daley Center★★

Bounded by Washington, Clark, Randolph & Dearborn Sts.

The Daley Center is probably best known for its plaza, where Picasso's fantastic steel creature holds court. Chicagoans shuddered at first, but the beast may now be as famous (and beloved) as "Hizzoner da Mare" himself, who governed the city from 1955 to 1976. Housing courtrooms and offices, this fine example of the International style of architecture was completed in 1965 (at the time, it was the city's tallest building). Seasonal festivities, topical rallies, protests, and a summertime farmers' market take place under the Picasso.

© Kim Karpeles/age fotostock

Richard J. Daley Center

Chicago Board of Trade Building★

141 W. Jackson Blvd. 312-435-7180.
www.cbotbuilding.com.

Hog futures, anyone? The Board of Trade was founded in 1848 to regulate trade of the Midwest's bountiful agricultural commodities. This outstanding Art Deco skyscraper (1930, Holabird & Root) testifies to that abundance, anchoring the south end of the LaSalle Street financial district. Ceres, the goddess of the harvest, gazes down from high atop the building's soaring roof. Today all the action takes place inside on the 60,000-square-foot trading floors, where frenetic traders in brightly colored jackets buy and sell stock options and commodities. But, even if you don't go inside, you can get a sense of the building's heft and significance by looking at how it anchors the canyon of skyscrapers on LaSalle Street.

Macy's State St.★

111 N. State St. 312-781-1000.
www.macys.com. Open year-round Mon–Fri 10am–8pm, Sat 9am–10pm, Sun 11am–6pm.
Closed major holidays.

This grand old department store occupies an entire block at the north end of fabled State Street. It was completed in stages between 1892 and 1914 by D.H. Burnham & Co., and its richly embellished corner clock remains a Chicago icon, despite the fact that the name changed from Marshall Field's to Macy's in 2006. The interior features over a million square feet of retail space and a lovely Tiffany favrile dome. If you're in town around the holidays, take in the legendary decorated windows and have lunch under the 45-foot Christmas tree in the Walnut Room restaurant, both traditions that Macy's kept intact.

State Street★

The song that made State Street— "that great street"—famous (*Chicago* by Fred Fisher) dates back to 1922, when merchants liked to call the intersection at State and Madison streets the "World's Busiest Corner." True or not, *everybody* crowded State Street in those days: shoppers, movie and theatergoers, office workers. But State Street had been great since the 1860s when real-estate magnate Potter Palmer bought a stretch of the muddy, narrow byway. He convinced the city council to widen it, replaced

Meals at Macy's

Macy's is a great place to go when you get hungry; the department store has a restaurant for every taste. On the 7th floor, the white-tablecloth **Walnut Room** (*312-781-3125*) conjures up bygone days when genteel gloved and hatted ladies lunched in the middle of their busy shopping day. You'll find a lighter lunch and soda-fountain desserts at the **Frango Café** (*312-781-2945*), where you can also buy Chicago's Frango mints, though Field's famous candies are no longer made here. **Seven on State** (*312-781-3693*) serves grilled Thai shrimp, ham crêpes and other upscale dishes in a sleek food-court setting. For burgers and pub fare, try **Infield's** (*800-634-3537*), where nonshoppers can catch up on their sports news.

MUST SEE

rundown shacks with the elegant Palmer House Hotel, and lured Field, Leiter, and Company from Lake Street by building them a new department store. Suddenly, State Street was *the* place to be. Though all was destroyed by the 1871 fire, the street came back with a vengeance. As you stroll the blocks between Wacker and Congress, look for signs recounting more State Street history (*www.chicagolooalliance.com*). Don't skip the 19C glamour of the 1895 **Reliance Building**★★ *(32 N. State St.)*, now reincarnated as the **Hotel Burnham** *(see p148)*. Its renovation makes it one of the few architectural treasures you can still see and appreciate from both the exterior and the interior.

MAGNIFICENT MILE★★★

The Champs Élysées of Chicago, this promenade along North Michigan Avenue, from the Chicago River north to Oak Street, is the city's most prestigious thoroughfare, blooming with plantings in the summer and twinkling with holiday lights all winter. Lined with exclusive boutiques and large retail stores, luxury hotels and premier residential and office high rises, the "Boul Mich" has come a long way from its beginnings as an ordinary city street. Its most distinctive relics survived the Great Fire in 1871; the bizarre 1869 Water Tower★ *(see p42)* still stands toward the north end at Chicago Avenue. The opening of the Michigan Avenue Bridge★ *(Wacker Dr. & N. Michigan Ave.)* joined the north and south sides of the city in 1920, igniting an incredible building boom that spawned most of the original landmarks on the avenue. The John Hancock Center★★★ *(see p38)* and Water Tower Place★ *(no. 835)* ushered in a new era of skyscrapers and retailing in the early 1970s when Michigan Avenue displaced State Street★ as the city's shopping corridor *(see pp26, 103)*.

Along the Boulevard

Sights below are arranged in geographical order, from south to north. See map, p28–29.

Wrigley Building★★

400–410 N. Michigan Ave.

Set majestically on the north side of the river, this sparkling structure was built in two stages (30 stories to the south in 1920 and 21 to the north in 1924, both designed by Graham, Anderson, Probst & White). The white terra-cotta exterior, its six subtle shades chosen to add more luster at the top, is particularly stunning when it's lit up at night.

©Chicago Architecture Foundation/Anne Evans

Wrigley Building

Tribune Tower★★

435 N. Michigan Ave.

Corporate headquarters of the Tribune Company's vast empire, this soaring tower (Hood & Howells), built in 1925, is a true "cathedral of commerce." Besides its dramatic Gothic style, the "Trib Tower" is known for the fragments and stones from the world's famous structures and sites that were collected by *Tribune* correspondents and embedded in its exterior walls. Look closely to find stones from the Berlin Wall, Omaha Beach, the Taj Mahal, and 117 others.

InterContinental Chicago★

505 N. Michigan Ave. 312-944-4100. www.interconti.com.
See p141.

The gold-leaf dome atop this 41-story building was a popular design among the Shriners, a Masonic fraternity, for whom the building was constructed as an athletics club in 1929. Step through its heavy bronze doors into a quasi-Eastern fantasia of design. Today's modern hotel (opened in 1990) retains the club's opulent oriental decoration. If you can, head up to the 14th floor to see the Olympic-size swimming pool, nestled under an opulently decorated ceiling.

Fourth Presbyterian Church★

N. Michigan Ave. at Delaware Pl. 312-787-4570. www.fourthchurch. org. Open year-round daily 9am–5pm. Closed major holidays.

Duck into this quiet sanctuary to escape Michigan Avenue's hustle

MAGNIFICENT MILE

Hotels
1. Allerton Crowne Plaza
2. Chicago's Lenox Suites Hotel
3. The Drake Hotel
4. Fitzpatrick Chicago
5. Four Seasons
6. InterContinental Chicago
7. Le Meridien
8. Millennium Knickerbocker Hotel
9. The Peninsula Chicago
10. The Raphael
11. Red Roof Inn
12. Seneca Hotel
13. Sofitel Chicago Water Tower
14. Talbott Hotel
15. The Tremont Hotel
16. W Chicago Lakeshore
17. The Whitehall Hotel

and bustle. Dedicated in 1914, the church is an elegant reminder of Michigan Avenue's bygone character. A blend of French and English Gothic styles, the church seats 1,500 people and is softly

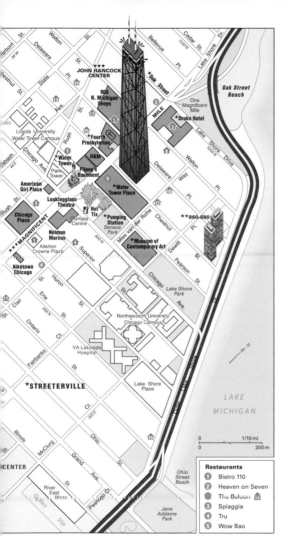

Restaurants
1. Bistro 110
2. Heaven on Seven
• The Saloon
3. Spiaggia
4. Tru
5. Wow Bao

lit by stunning medieval-style stained-glass windows. Controversy has swirled around the high-rise condominiums planned adjacent to this lovely place of worship.

Oak Street★

Between N. Michigan Ave. & Rush St. See p103.

One of the city's swankiest streets, Oak Street is worthy of a stroll, even

© City of Chicago / GRC

The Magnificent Mile Lights Festival

Chicagoans love festivals and fireworks, and not just in the summer. Michigan Avenue dresses up for the holidays on the weekend before Thanksgiving with the Magnificent Mile Lights Festival. A Saturday of music, ice carving and performances up and down the avenue culminates with the illumination of more than a million twinkling lights and a parade led by Mickey Mouse.

Fireworks over the Chicago River end the evening with a bang. Stores are open late if you want to get a jump on your holiday shopping. *www.themagnificentmile.com.*

if you don't intend to shop. As you would on Rodeo Drive or Madison Avenue, you may want to dress the part before hitting the sidewalk. Restaurants and bars balance out the boutiques for non-shoppers.

The Drake Hotel★

140 E. Walton St. 312-787-2200. www.thedrakehotel.com. See p140.

Grand dame of Chicago's luxury hotels, the Drake retains its 1920s atmosphere. At the top of Michigan Avenue, it overlooks Oak Street Beach and Lake Shore Drive. Admire the plush red-velvet wall coverings, the wooden caisson

ceiling, and the elegant **Palm Court** in the dignified lobby. No visit to the Drake is complete without **English-style high tea** *(daily 1–5pm; reservations recommended)*.

Sip Darjeeling tea amid lush plantings and silken furniture, nibbling on tiny sandwiches, scones, and clotted cream.

Museum of Contemporary Art★
See p54. *220 E. Chicago Ave.*

American Girl Place
See p100. *111 E. Chicago Ave.*

Streeterville★

Between the lake and North Michigan Avenue, **Streeterville** was settled in the 1880s by Capt. George Streeter, who declared it the "District of Lake Michigan," separate from the city of Chicago. Bounded on the south by the Chicago River, the area is the home of Northwestern University's Chicago campus and the residential towers at **860–880 North Lake Shore Drive★★**, which established the high-rise influence of modern architect Ludwig Mies van der Rohe in the early 1950s. To the east lies **Navy Pier★★** *(see pp15, 87, 97).*

RIVER NORTH★★

Between the Chicago River & North Branch, and Oak St. & Michigan Ave.
www.rivernorthassociation.com.

Bounded on the west and south by the Chicago River, this neighborhood includes Wolf Point at the river's bend, one of Chicago's oldest areas of settlement. Early industries and shantytowns established themselves along the river, while the northeast corner sprouted mansions and cathedrals. Over the decades, working-class, immigrant, bohemian, and wealthy residents staked claims around this neighborhood, which now claims many of the city's best galleries, restaurants, and nightclubs.

Newberry Library★★

60 W. Walton St. 312-943-9090.
www.newberry.org. Reading
rooms open year-round Tue–Thu
10am–6pm, Fri–Sat 9am–5pm.
Closed major holidays.

Want to look up your family tree? This respected institution, completed in 1893, ranks among the top independent research libraries in the country for genealogists and scholars in the humanities. Rotating exhibits— on such diverse topics as *Alice in Wonderland* and King Arthur— draw heavily on the library's collections and offer the general public an opportunity to sample the rare book, manuscript, and map treasures. A look around the lobby will give you a good sense of the building's grandeur.

Marina City★

300 N. State St.

From the river's edge rise the twin "corncob" towers of Bertrand Goldberg's experimental urban community. Revolutionary when conceived in 1959, the complex, which includes apartments as well as entertainment and services, was an attempt to encourage young professionals to settle in the city. The Marina Towers' cast-concrete

Gallery Hopping in River North
The **River North Gallery District** *(see p107)* spans an eight-square-block area in River North. You'll find dozens of galleries here exhibiting an array of styles and media. On certain Friday evenings each month *(5–8pm)*, the galleries open their new shows *(for schedules, check online at www.chicagogallerynews.com or pick up a free copy of Chicago Gallery News).*

construction and rippling surfaces contrast dramatically with the "glass boxes" so popular at the time.

Merchandise Mart
See p106. 300 N. Wells St.

Newberry Library
©Newberry Library

GOLD COAST★

Between Oak St. & North Ave., and extending west from the lake to LaSalle St.
This slice of Chicago's lakefront has been home to the city's well-to-do for more than a century. While all but a few of the mansions that once lined Lake Shore Drive have been demolished, you can still step back a century with a walk along State Parkway and landmark **Astor Street★★**, where quaint Victorian town houses and elegant Renaissance-inspired graystones occupy tiny, beautifully cultivated lots.

Chicago Architecture Foundation Tours

Throughout the year, knowledgeable docents at the Chicago Architecture Foundation (CAF) lead 78 different neighborhood walks. And lest you feel timid about architecture, fear not. These excellent tours make stone and steel come alive, and you'll meet some of Chicago's most interesting characters along the way. For schedules and fees, contact CAF headquarters at the **ArchiCenter** *(224 S. Michigan Ave.; 312-922-3432, ext. 240; www.architecture.org).*

Charnley-Persky House★

1365 Astor St., at Schiller St. 312-915-0105. www.sah.org; www.charnleyhouse.org. Visit by one-hour guided tour only year-round Wed at noon (free). Sat tours offered Apr–Nov 10am & 1pm, Dec–Mar 10am ($5).

With its plain brick and limestone façade and horizontal form, the Charnley-Persky House stands out amid the Victorian residential architecture that was popular at the turn of the 20C. Architect Louis Sullivan (with some input by his draftsman Frank Lloyd Wright) designed the house in 1892 for lumberman James Charnley. Inside, 11 rooms surround a central atrium; the kitchen is located in the narrow basement.

Oak Street Beach
See p91. Lake Shore Dr. at Oak St.

Houses on Astor Street

© Kim Karpeles / Alamy

ANDERSONVILLE

Bounded by Winnemac & Elmdale Aves., and Ravenswood & Magnolia Aves.

In the 19C, Swedish immigrant farmers were drawn to this outlying community because it was one of the few areas where poorer landowners could build wooden, instead of more expensive brick or stone, homes. Now a central fixture of the city's North Side, Andersonville kept its Swedish roots, but is also home to a thriving gay and lesbian population, and an eclectic mix of other city-dwellers. Andersonville is dotted with great restaurants (Swedish and otherwise), home-décor boutiques, and dance and nightclubs.

Clark Street
See p104.

Swedish-American Museum Center
See p104. **5211 N. Clark St.**

LITTLE SAIGON

Argyle Ave. between Broadway & Sheridan Rd.

Just southeast of Andersonville, by a matter of blocks, is the tiny heart of the city's Vietnamese community. You'll know you've arrived when you see the uniquely topped Asian-style El station that spans Argyle Avenue. (If you can, take the El here and exit at this stop. Parking in the neighborhood can be a challenge.) Some locals refer to this area as "New Chinatown," because of its multi-Asian influences and to distinguish it from the South Side's Chinatown *(see p36)*. While it is small, this community is active and crowded day and night. Come here hungry, as every block is packed with small Pho shops and other authentic Vietnamese restaurants and grocery stores. You'll also find solid Thai, Japanese, and Chinese eateries, including some dim sum brunches on the weekends.

LINCOLN SQUARE

Northwest of downtown. Lincoln Ave, bounded by Montrose and Lawrence Aves.

As Andersonville was the historic neighborhood for Swedish immigrants, Lincoln Square (not to be confused with Lincoln Park, *see p65*) was home to the city's many German settlers. The highlight of Lincoln Square is the brick-lined, pedestrian-friendly stretch of Lincoln Ave., between Leland and Lawrence Aves. Here you'll find pastry shops, bookstores, toy stores, and outdoor plazas with live music (when weather permits). Many high-end Lakeview bars and restaurants have migrated to Lincoln Square in recent years, making the neighborhood a hot spot for nightlife, either before or after a concert at the Old Town School of Folk Music *(4544 N. Lincoln Ave.; 773-728-6000; www.oldtown school.org).*

NEIGHBORHOODS

33

Sulzer Regional Library

4455 N. Lincoln Ave.

More than a mere branch of the public library, Sulzer (named after one of the neighborhood's first residents) is a destination for those who want to research Chicago's history, thanks to a unique collection of source materials.

Furnishings were custom-designed to reflect the neighborhood's German roots.

Old Town School of Folk Music
4544 N. Lincoln Ave.
Former library hosts classes, performances, and events in a 420-seat auditorium. Paired with original site at 909 W. Armitage.

OLD TOWN★
Bounded by Division, Halsted & LaSalle Sts., and Armitage Ave.
Working-class German families settled this area in the 1840s and 50s, and by 1900, North Avenue—the German Broadway—was alive with shops, bakeries, taverns, and delicatessens. In the early 20C, as the Germans moved north, the neighborhood fell into disrepair. It remained largely so until the low rents began to attract an artistic clientele in the mid-19C. In 1959 The Second City comedy improv theater *(see p118)* **took root here. The area's funky reputation lingered into the 1990s, now having all but disappeared as the 21C ushered in a retail and residential building boom in Old Town and environs. Take a walk through Old Town Triangle (bounded roughly by North & Lincoln Aves.) to get a sense of the way people lived in the 1800s.**

Menomonee Street★
The 300 block of this quaint street is the essence of Old Town. Nine cottages, **nos. 325–345**, are good examples of the small wooden cottages originally built here; they could be erected in no time using "balloon framing." This building innovation was accountable for the rapid growth and combustibility of the city. The tiny house at no. 216 is a rare example of a fire-relief shanty, a one-room dwelling built with funds donated by the Chicago Fire Relief and Aid Society for families left homeless by the fire. Also visible on the street are early 20C structures that once housed automobiles and chauffeurs for Gold Coast residents, now converted into living units.

Old Town Art Fair

A neighborhood fund-raising initiative begun in 1947 evolved into the Old Town Art Fair, which today draws thousands of art lovers to the area just north of North Avenue the second weekend in June. The premier fair features more than 250 artists, a silent jewelry auction, food, music, and more *($5 donation requested). For more information, contact the Old Town Triangle Association: 312-337-1938 or www.oldtownartfair.org.*

Chicago History Museum★
See p54. 1600 North Ave.

PILSEN

Southwest of downtown, from the Chicago River west to the city limits.

Pilsen started out in the 19C as the largest settlement of Bohemian immigrants in the country. Over the years, Germans, Irish, Polish, and Lithuanians passed through here, and today Pilsen forms the core of Chicago's enormous Hispanic population. The neighborhood, which centers on Halsted and 18th streets, also attracts artists, who open their studios in late September or early October each year for the Pilsen East Artists Open House *(312-738-8000)*. You can see much of Pilsen's art, however—in the form of large, colorful murals—on any excursion down 18th Street. Taquerias, markets, and shops line the street as well; stop by Restaurante Nuevo Leon *(1515 W. 18th St.; 312-421-1517)* for a delicious traditional Mexican meal served in a family atmosphere. In late July, the Fiesta del Sol livens up the blocks from Throop to Morgan streets with outdoor music, food, and fun *(312-666-2663; www.fiestadelsol.org)*.

National Museum of Mexican Art
1852 W. 19th St. See p58.

BUCKTOWN AND WICKER PARK

Northwest of downtown, from the Chicago River west to Western Ave., and Webster Ave. & Division St.

What SoHo was to Manhattan, Bucktown and Wicker Park were to Chicago. These adjacent neighborhoods (often lumped together as one) attracted creatively rich but cash-poor designers and artists in the late 1980s and early 90s, thanks to big, open loft spaces with low rents. As was the case in SoHo, artists soon got priced out of their affordable neighborhood, but the artsy vibe remains. This is one of the city's best areas for boutique shopping, happening nightlife, interesting restaurants, and excellent people-watching.

Flat Iron Arts Building

1579 N. Milwaukee Ave.

The 1913 Greek Revival building that occupies the triangle at the corner of Damen and Milwaukee Aves. is the geographic and emotional heart of these neighborhoods. Originally designed by architects Holabird & Roche, today it is home to more than 30 artists' studios. It is also ground zero for Around the Coyote, the neighborhood's twice-annual art crawl-cum-street festival, now the largest collection of open studios, galleries, and arts-related events in the city, spanning a mile or more in each direction from the "Coyote" Tower, a 1928 design by Chatten Perkins and Hammond.

Damen and Milwaukee Avenues
See p105.

NEIGHBORHOODS

BRIDGEPORT, BRONZEVILLE, AND CHINATOWN

South of downtown, both sides of the I 90-94 Expressway, south to 35th St.

This trio is a melting pot of South Side neighborhoods. Bridgeport was traditionally the neighborhood in which Irish immigrants settled. But today it is better known for two things: Being home to the Daley political clan and also to the US Cellular Field, where the Chicago White Sox play baseball. Bronzeville was one of the most significant neighborhoods in African-American history. Many of the buildings in the neighborhood were built and financed by African-American capital during the neighborhood's heydey in the early 20C. After suffering from neglect, the neighborhood is enjoying a resurgence. Nearby Chinatown pales in geographic size to the likes of those in San Francisco or New York. What the area lacks in physical stature, though, it makes up for in diversity of offerings.

🏛 Blues Heaven

2120 S. Michigan Ave. 312-808-1286. www.bluesheaven.com.

The former home to Chess Records Office and Studios is where classics like *Red Rooster* and *Johnny B Goode* were recorded. Take a tour of this spot, which is now home to Blues Heaven, and you can almost hear legends like Muddy Waters, Willie Dixon, and the Rolling Stones in the ether. **Tours** include the main studio and rehearsal spaces.

Chinese-American Museum of Chicago
See p55. 238 W. 23rd St.

Illinois Institute of Technology (IIT)★

3201 S. State St. 312-567-5014. www.iit.edu.

The IIT campus realizes the vision of master Modernist architect **Ludwig Mies van der Rohe** (1886–1969), who directed the school's architecture program after fleeing Nazi Germany. There are a number of worthy buildings on campus.

Among those that are not-to-be-missed are **S.R. Crown Hall★★** and **Carr Memorial Chapel**. Crown Hall is the crowning achievement for both Mies van der Rohe and IIT, with its glass-walled pavilion and dramatic flat roof. Carr is the only church ever designed by Mies. Dutch architect **Rem Koolhaas** challenged the Miesian tradition in 2005 with the funky **McCormick Tribune Campus Center★**.

US Cellular Field

333 W. 35th St. 312-674-1000. whitesox.mlb.com.

The Cubs' **Wrigley Field★** *(see p43)* gets all the love, but this home to the Chicago White Sox is not a bad place to see a baseball game. The stadium replaced the old Comiskey Park in 1991. What "The Cell" lacks in charm it makes up for in creature comforts, such as more spacious seating and concession stands that have vegetarian-friendly options. Plus, the Sox put on an excellent fireworks display after many games.

LAKEVIEW

Bounded by Lake Michigan west to Ashland Ave. and Fullerton Ave. & Irving Park Rd.

Home to Wrigley Field★, Belmont Harbor, and scores of 20-somethings who have recently moved to Chicago from college towns across the country, Lakeview is one of the most active—and crowded—of the North Side neighborhoods, filled with apartments and three-flats for young professionals. Come here to enjoy live music, live baseball, and 24-7 energy. Just don't drive: Parking is all but impossible!

Hutchinson Street District★
See p72. Between Lake Shore Dr & Hazel St.

Southport Avenue
See p104. Bounded by Belmont Ave. & Irving Park Rd.

Wrigley Field★
See p43. 1060 W. Addison St.

HYDE PARK

South of downtown, bounded by Lake Michigan west to Cottage Grove Ave., and on 49th St & 60th St.

Best known as home to the University of Chicago★★, Hyde Park is the South Side neighborhood even North Siders love. Whether you are an architecture fan, an academic, or a shopper, you'll be able to spend hours here strolling the leafy streets and mansions of Kenwood (home to President Obama!), enjoying the Gothic campus, where the buildings mimic the landmarks of Oxford and Cambridge, or finding rare treasures among the cottages and boutiques of 547th Street.

Museum of Science and Industry★★★
See pp48, 95. 57th St., at S. Lake Shore Dr.

Oriental Institute★★
See p53. 1155 E. 58th St.

Elijah Muhammad House

4855 S. Woodlawn Ave.

You can't miss the Mediterranean Modern style of this 1971 house, as it is so distinct from the rest of the 19C style of the area. You also are unlikely to miss it as it will be surrounded by guards, either on foot or in cars, whether you walk by day or night.
The house is home to the Nation of Islam leader, and is under constant watch. Admire the stained-glass windows and red-tiled roof. Across the street you'll see similar, albeit smaller, homes that were built for Muhammad's son.

Robie House★★
See p71. 5757 S. Woodlawn Ave.

LANDMARKS

Chicago has few towering monuments or hallowed spaces. This is a practical city where the most important landmarks are working buildings in busy neighborhoods. Indeed, the city of Chicago has conferred "landmark status" on 203 individual sites and 36 districts, from the Black Metropolis-Bronzeville District on the South Side to the Uptown Theater on the north. Besides these literal landmarks, however, certain icons say "Chicago" around the world.

John Hancock Center★★★

875 N. Michigan Ave.

Muscular and monumental, nothing says Chicago like the profile of "Big John." Built in 1969 (Skidmore, Owings & Merrill), the 100-story tower is a city unto itself, with 2.8 million square feet housing retail, restaurant, office, and residential space. These homes were the highest in the world . . . until they were "trumped" by the Trump Tower, which, when it opened in 2008 on the north bank of the Chicago River, offered luxury condos that are even higher.

The Hancock tower's tapering frame is crisscrossed by brawny braces, which eliminate the need for inner support beams, greatly enlarging the usable space inside. Made of some 46,000 tons of steel, the building can easily withstand gravity and wind. It's lovely at night, when a band of lights girdles the heights of the building in festive holiday color or plain bright white.

Walk around to the west side of the building's base and follow the wide steps down into a large sunken plaza framing colorful planters and a waterfall. From the plaza you'll have interesting views of the

John Hancock Center

©Chicago Architecture Foundation/Anne Evans

High-altitude Dining: Signature Room at the 95th

For breathtaking views of the lake and Navy Pier, with food to match, take the elevator up to the Signature Room on the 95th floor *(312-787-9596; www.sig natureroom.com)*. The lavish lunch buffet (or you can order off the menu) is a treat, and dinnertime offerings include well-prepared seafood and hearty meat dishes. If you're not up for an expensive dinner, go up one floor to the **Signature Lounge at the 96th** for 360-degree panoramas, a bit of jazz, and a specialty martini. Or perhaps a nightcap and dessert. Dress is "upscale casual."

MUST SEE

surrounding Mag Mile skyscrapers and a sheltered place to soak up the sun and enjoy a cup of coffee.

The Hancock Observatory

On the 94th floor of the John Hancock Center. 888-875-8439. www.hancock-observatory.com. Open daily 9am–11pm (last ticket sold at 10:45pm). $16.80 adults, $11.20 children (free for children under age 3).

During the 39 seconds that the elevator takes to ascend to the 94th floor, your ears will pop and your stomach will drop. Once there, however, the panoramic **views★★★** of lake and landscape in every direction are well worth the ride. On a clear day, you'll see four states: Illinois, Indiana, Wisconsin, and Michigan, and, of course, the blue expanse of Lake Michigan that stretches east and north. The open-air **Skywalk**, the highest balcony in America, allows visitors to experience the weather a thousand feet up, regardless of the Chicago weather (prepare for wind). Other attractions, such as a history wall, recorded tours, and talking telescopes, are fun and informative, but let's face it—it's the view that counts.

Willis Tower (formerly Sears Tower)★★★

233 S. Wacker Dr.

Tallest building in the world for more than 20 years, this 110-story feat of engineering cuts an unmistakable profile on the city's skyline. At the time of its construction, from 1968 to 1974, the city did not require a zoning variance for the tower, allowing it to rise to an unsurpassed height of

1,450 feet. Since 1996, the tower has thrice been topped as the world's tallest building; first by the Petronas Towers in Kuala Lumpur, Malaysia, then in 2003 by Taipei 101 in Taipei, Taiwan, and most recently by Burj Khalifa in Dubai. The Willis Tower still holds the title of world's tallest building to the tips of its antennae, and it remains—so far— the tallest building in the US. It may also be the deepest. Designed by Skidmore, Owings & Merrill, one of the most influential architectural firms of the 20C, the Willis Tower (renamed in 2009) is composed of nine rectangular tubes resting on more than 100 steel and concrete caissons anchored into the bedrock hundreds of feet below ground. These 75-foot-high bundled tubes provide maximum resistance to high winds; two tubes end at the 50th floor, two at the 66th floor, and three more at the 90th floor. Clad in black aluminum and bronze-tinted glass, the tower's structural skeleton required more than 75,000 tons of steel.

©Chicago Architecture Foundation/Anne Evans

Sears Tower

Chicago's Watermark

Of course, the biggest landmark (watermark, really) in the city spreads out from its doorstep over 22,000 square miles. That would be **Lake Michigan**, and it is an awe-inspiring sight. The name comes from an Algonquian word meaning "big lake," but actually, Michigan is but the third largest of the five Great Lakes and the only one completely within US borders.

At nearly 1,000 feet at its deepest, the lake never freezes all the way across—a distance of about 30 miles at the southern end. To get a real sense of Lake Michigan, take a walk along the lakefront from Navy Pier to the Museum Campus. The lake's moods change daily, but it is always beautiful.

Check out the barrel-vaulted entrance on Wacker Drive, where sculptor Alexander Calder's mobile **The Universe**, a collection of brightly colored forms, turns and twirls. Despite the attraction's popularity, the lines to the top generally move quickly, and new glass boxes allow you to look 103 stories straight down below your feet!

Tower Facts

+ Even in high wind, the top of the Sears Tower never sways more than six inches.
+ The tower weighs in at 222,500 tons, and it's covered by 28 acres of black aluminum.

Buckingham Fountain★★
*See p64. Columbus Dr.,
at Congress Pkwy. in Grant Park.*

Marquette Building★★

*140 S. Dearborn St. 312-726-8000.
www.macfound.org.*

The MacArthur Foundation bought and renovated this landmark building and now offers a free exhibit *(Mon–Fri 7am–6pm, Sat-Sun 9am–6pm)* about this early skyscraper's magnificent details inside and out. Make sure to see the lobby, with its Tiffany tile mosaic and bronze busts of Native Americans and explorers.

Tall Tales

If size matters to you, here's how the Sears Tower and "Big John" stack up:

	Willi (Sears)	John Hancock
Height	1,450 feet without antennae	1,127 feet
Stories	110	100
Weight	222,500 tons	192,000 tons
Square feet	4.5 million	2.8 million
Elevators	103	50
Top elevator speed	1,600 feet per minute	1,800 feet per minute
Number of windows	16,100	11,459
Steps to the top	2,232	1,632

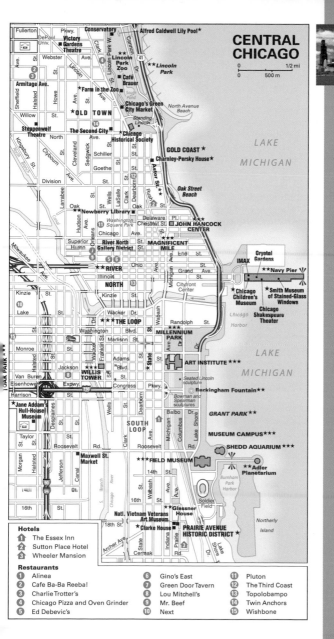

CENTRAL CHICAGO

0 ____ 1/2 mi
0 ____ 500 m

Alfred Caldwell Lily Pool★

Conservatory★

★★ **Lincoln Park Zoo**

★★ *Lincoln Park*

■ **Café Brauer**

★ **Farm in the Zoo**

■ **Chicago's Green City Market**

★ **OLD TOWN**

North Avenue Beach

Victory Gardens Theatre

Steppenwolf Theatre

The Second City

★ **Chicago Historical Society**

GOLD COAST ★

■ **Charnley-Persky House★**

Oak Street Beach

★★ **Newberry Library**

Washington Square Park ■

★★★ **JOHN HANCOCK CENTER**

★★ **River North Gallery District**

MAGNIFICENT MILE

★★ **RIVER NORTH**

Crystal Gardens

IMAX

★★ **Navy Pier** ⚓

★ **Chicago Children's Museum**

★ **Smith Museum of Stained-Glass Windows**

Chicago Shakespeare Theater

Cityfront Center

★★★ **THE LOOP**

★★★ **MILLENNIUM PARK**

Willis Tower ★★★

★ **State St.**

ART INSTITUTE ★★★

Seated Lincoln sculpture

★ **Jane Addams Hull-House Museum**

SOUTH LOOP

Bowman and Spearman sculptures

Buckingham Fountain★★

GRANT PARK ★★

MUSEUM CAMPUS★★★

SHEDD AQUARIUM ★★★

■ **Maxwell St. Market**

★★★ **FIELD MUSEUM**

★★ **Adler Planetarium**

Burnham Park Harbor

Soldier Field

Northerly Island

Natl. Vietnam Veterans Art Museum

★★ **Glessner House**

■ **Clarke House**

PRAIRIE AVENUE HISTORIC DISTRICT ★

LAKE MICHIGAN

Chicago Harbor

Hotels
1. The Essex Inn
2. Sutton Place Hotel
3. Wheeler Mansion

Restaurants
1. Alinea
2. Cafe Ba-Ba-Reeba!
3. Charlie Trotter's
4. Chicago Pizza and Oven Grinder
5. Ed Debevic's
6. Gino's East
7. Green Door Tavern
8. Lou Mitchell's
9. Mr. Beef
10. Next
11. Pluton
12. The Third Coast
13. Topolobampo
14. Twin Anchors
15. Wishbone

Chicago River Tours

The Chicago River flows backwards from Lake Michigan (engineers reversed its flow in 1900 to keep waste out of the lake, the source of the city's drinking water). The river is now spanned by some 52 movable bridges, each one an engineering marvel. Condos and restaurants line its banks, the pleasant **Riverwalk★** winds along beside it, and great works of urban architecture loom above it. To enjoy these vistas, take a Chicago Architecture Foundation **Architecture River Cruise**. The 90-minute tours depart at least six times daily, rain or shine, from May 1 to the end of November from the dock located at the southeast corner of the Michigan Avenue Bridge and Wacker Drive *(reservations recommended: 312-902-1500; for details, contact the Architecture Foundation: 312-922-3432 or www.architecture.org).*

Navy Pier★★

*See pp15, 87, 97. **600 E. Grand Ave., at Lake Michigan.***

Chicago Water Tower and Pumping Station★

On either side of N. Michigan Ave., at Chicago Ave.

In 1850s Chicago, contaminated water took its toll on human health and city development. In 1855 city sewage commissioners decided to bring in fresh lake water by building a tunnel extending two miles out under Lake Michigan.

A huge water intake "crib" (50 feet by 70 feet) was built on land and floated out to be firmly grounded into the lake bottom at a depth of 40 feet. (From the shoreline, you can see the original crib's successors up and down the lakefront.) A tunnel was then built 6 feet under the lakebed to connect the crib with the pumping station and provide the city with fresh water from the lake. Ridiculed by naysayers, the plan came to be recognized as a masterpiece of engineering. Now dwarfed by high rises, the castle-like structures

Chicago Water Tower

©Chicago Architecture Foundation/Anne Evans

Billy Goat's Curse

It started when William Sianis and his billy goat, Murphy, were ejected from Game 4 of the World Series at Wrigley Field in 1945. "Cubs, they not gonna win anymore," Sianis vowed. The team lost the series and never returned. Though attempts have been made to lift the curse by allowing Murphy's descendants into Wrigley, it endures. As does Sianis' **Billy Goat Tavern** *(430 N. Michigan Ave., lower level; 312-222-1525).* The subterranean tavern (now run by Sianis' nephew, Sam) offers a real, greasy slice of Chicago history.

MUST SEE

of the Chicago Water Tower and Pumping Station (built in the late 1860s) were the only two public buildings to survive the 1871 fire. Today a lovely park surrounds the tower, while the pumping station, though still operational, has been refitted as the home of **Lookingglass Theatre** *(312-337-0665; www.lookingglasstheatre.org)*. The building is a frequent meeting place for Mag Mile tourists.

Wrigley Field★

1060 W. Addison St. 773-404-2827. www.chicago.cubs.com. For ticket information, see p89.

Built as Weeghman Field In 1914 for the Chicago Whales of the Federal League before being occupied by the Cubs of the National League two years later, this stadium is an icon for baseball lovers everywhere. It's the oldest surviving National League ballpark and second only to Boston's Fenway Park (1912) overall. The Chicago Bears played football here from their beginnings in 1921 until 1970 before moving to Soldier Field in 1971. Famous for its ivy walls and lovable losing teams, the stadium is surrounded by early 20C flats rather than the usual sea of parking lots. Many of the adjacent buildings boast rooftop clubs where ticket buyers watch the game over the outfield walls. The first night game was played here in 1988 after a long battle with neighbors to keep lights out of the field, and a more recent renovation extended the outfield walls and added seating to the beloved landmark.

Skydeck

Enter on Jackson Blvd., between Wacker Dr. & Franklin St. 312-875-9696. www.theskydeck.com. Open May–Sept 10am–10pm. Rest of the year 10am–8pm. $17 adults, $11 children.

Elevators blast off to the top of the Willis Tower at 1,600 feet per minute. When you land on the Skydeck, 103 stories up, an awesome **view★★★** (on a clear day) for 50 miles around greets you. New "Ledge" glass boxes allow you to look straight down 1,353 feet! Exhibits, telescopes, and kid-level views help you pick out sites.

City of Chicago/Chris McGuire

Wrigley Field

MUSEUMS

Chicago takes justifiable pride in its array of museums; indeed, you could spend a week and not do them all justice. Some command majestic profiles on the lakefront; others grace parks and neighborhoods around the city. From earthly fossils to celestial bodies, Chicago's museums can indulge most any cultural pleasure.

Modern Wing, The Art Institute of Chicago

©The Art Institute of Chicago

Art Institute of Chicago★★★

111 S. Michigan Ave. 312-443-3600. www.artinstituteof chicago.org. Open year-round Mon–Fri 10:30am–4:30pm (Thu free 5–8pm), Sat–Sun 10am–5pm. Closed Thanksgiving Day, Christmas Day, and New Year's Day. $18 adults; $12 children (free for children ages 12 and under). Free admission first and second Wednesday each month.

One of the great museums of the world and the preeminent arts institution of the Midwest, the Art Institute of Chicago (AIC) is a comprehensive center for arts education and exhibition. Its collections span 5,000 years and draw on the cultures of Europe, Asia, Africa, and the Americas. If you're a lover of the Impressionist

Eat Your Art Out

For a quick sandwich, grill selection, pizza, or salad (and best for kids), visit the self-service **Café** on the lower level. The **Garden Restaurant** *(lower level; 312-553-9675)* features table service, a full bar, and a menu of contemporary American and seafood dishes. During the summer, the restaurant flings wide its doors onto the shady McKinlock Court for alfresco dining. Enter at Columbus Drive if you are only dining.

period, this is the place for you: the museum's reputation rests primarily on its collection of Impressionist and post-Impressionist paintings, one of the largest and most important outside France. Immerse yourself in a gallery or two, or sample a variety of the institute's visual delights. Founded as one of the first art schools in the US In 1866 (the School of the Art Institute remains a world-class facility), the AIC was reorganized to include a museum in 1879. The grand **World's Columbian Exposition** of 1893 provided the perfect opportunity for trustees to construct the glorious temple of art that stands on Michigan Avenue today, guarded by the bronze lions cast by sculptor Edward Kemeys in 1894. From the 50,000 square feet of the original Allerton Building, the institute has expanded to encompass more than 400,000 square feet, spanning the block between Michigan Avenue and Columbus Drive.

A new, $300-million, 65,000 square-foot Modern Wing designed by Renzo Piano opened in 2009 and is linked to Millennium Park by the Nichols Bridge.

Heart of the Art Institute

European Painting and Sculpture★★ – Medieval, Renaissance, and Baroque masterpieces occupy the entire second floor of the Allerton Building. They trace the

Detail of Nighthawks (1942) by Edward Hopper

Art Institute of Chicago, Friends of American Art Collection

MUSEUMS

development of Western painting from flat medieval landscapes to the flamboyance of the Rococo. Don't miss works by Botticelli, Rembrandt, and El Greco.

19C European Painting★★★ – From Goya to Gauguin, these galleries in upper Gunsaulus Hall sparkle with painterly genius. Check out the breathtaking array of Impressionists and post-Impressionist iconic masterpieces by Seurat, Monet, Van Gogh, Toulouse-Lautrec, and more. This collection was freshly reinstalled summer 2008.

The Modern Wing★★ – The new galleries in the Modern Wing house the collections of modern art, contemporary art, photography, and architecture and design. This is the largest expansion in the Art Institute's history, showcasing as never before the museum's commitment to emerging art, new technology, and modernity. Opens to the public May 16, 2009.

American Art★★ – Beginning with a delightful gallery of folk art, these exhibits chronicle the development of American taste through furniture, decorative arts, paintings, and sculpture. Iconic masterpieces

such as Grant Wood's *American Gothic* and Edward Hopper's *Nighthawks* can be found in this recently reinstalled presentation of the collection.

European Decorative Arts★★ – This collection is a trove of household, decorative, and religious objects produced since AD 1100. Check out the delectable **Rubloff Paperweight Collection★**, which looks good enough to eat.

Asian Art★★★ – In addition to a stunning collection of Chinese, Japanese, and Korean ancient artifacts, visitors should stroll through the Alsdorf Galleries of Indian and Southeast Asian Sculptures—a newly reinstalled, daylit space with an amazing view of the Chicago skyline.

Field Museum of Natural History★★★

1400 S. Lake Shore Dr. 312-922-9410. www.fieldmuseum.org. Open year-round daily 9am–5pm (last entry 4pm). Closed Dec 25. $22 adults, $12 children ages 4–11 (free for children 3 and under). Admission is discounted for Chicago residents.

This world-class natural history institution occupies a suitably grand place at the south end of Grant Park. Known as the **Museum Campus★★★**, this area also includes the **Shedd Aquarium★★★** and the **Adler Planetarium★★**. Nine acres of exhibit halls and over 20 million artifacts await you in the temple-like building completed in 1921 by architect Daniel Burnham. Dinosaur bones, artifacts from cultures around the world, and animal taxidermy have all been incorporated into fun, modern exhibits, though some galleries await updating. Even if only four percent of the collections are on exhibit when you go, there's still plenty to see!

A Dino Named Sue★★ –

The museum's famous *Tyranno-saurus rex* skeleton occupies the place of honor on the main floor in Stanley Field Hall. You can't miss Sue—she's 13 feet tall at the hip with a menacing grin! For more on Sue and her ilk, visit the second-floor galleries just above her. There you'll be able to get a close look at her actual skull, which, weighing in at 600 pounds, is too heavy to display on the skeleton.

Outstanding in the Field

Africa★★– This kaleidoscopic exhibit ventures from the streets of Dakar, Senegal, to the sand dunes of the Sahara. The sweeping presentation investigates African politics, art, environment, wildlife, commerce, and family life by highlighting the diverse cultures of the continent.

Eskimos and Northwest Coast Indians★★ –

A seemingly endless display of masks, totem poles, articles of clothing, and other Native American artifacts contrasts life in the Arctic and the Northwest.

Dino Zone★★ – At this exhibit you can touch dinosaur bones and teeth, and test your knowledge of dino trivia. The exhibit incorporates the newest scientific research about early life on Earth. There is a hands-on interpretive station, and in the McDonald's Fossil Preparation Lab you can watch fossils being prepared.

Hall of Gems★ – All love these shimmering precious and semiprecious stones, lusciously illuminated in a small darkened space.

Tyrannosaurus rex, *"Sue"*

© The Field Museum

Visiting MSI: This can be a hard museum to navigate efficiently because of its size and layout. Grab a floor plan and purchase entry, special-exhibit, and **Omnimax** tickets as you enter the Great Hall from the underground garage. Plan to see the **Coal Mine★★**, **Idea Factory**, and **U-505 Submarine★** early, as lines for these can develop fast. In the Great Hall, you can check your coat and rent a stroller before you ascend the escalator, elevators, or stairs to the ground level. Exhibits, restrooms and a cafeteria can be found on this floor. From here, the museum complex takes in the **Henry Crown Space Center** and three floors within the central, east, and west pavilions. The floors are connected by four color-coded stairwells off the rotunda of the central pavilion. East of the central pavilion, the Crown Center connects to the pavilions by a hallway accessible from the ground floor.

Nature Walk★ – The specimens and dioramas at the Field are second to none; they take you on a trek through woods, wetlands, and other wild places.

Plants of the World★ – This display will dazzle you with the incredible variety of form, color, and function of the world's plants.

Traveling the Pacific★ and **Pacific Spirits★** – These adjacent exhibits showcase the museum's collections from the cultures of the South Pacific. The highlight is the 1881 **Maori meeting house**, moved from New Zealand and reconstructed here piece by piece.

Underground Adventure★ – *Extra charge.* Walk among the creepy crawlies that live beneath our feet (simulated, of course) and get a bug's-eye view of life in the dirt.

Museum of Science and Industry★★★

57th St., at S. Lake Shore Dr. 773-684-1414. www.msichicago.org. Open year-round daily 9:30am–4pm, Closed Dec 25. $15 adults, $14 seniors, $10 children (ages 3–11). Free admission days vary by season. Additional charge for Omnimax Theater & special exhibits.

This noisy hall of wonders and widgets is one of Chicago's

U-505 Submarine, Museum of Science and Industry

Scott Brownell/Museum of Science and Industry

MUST SEE

most popular attractions, and the crowds prove it. Since 1933, the "MSI" has occupied the only building left standing after the **World's Columbian Exposition** of 1893 *(see p67)*. Designed in the grand Classical style by Charles B. Atwood as the Palace of Fine Arts (now the **Museum of Science and Industry★★★**), the building fell into disrepair until 1926 when the idea to house an "industrial" museum there took root. Over the years the museum has collected an amazing array of oddities and artifacts—from a miniature **Fairy Castle★**

to the world's fastest car. Today, spread out over four floors, the MSI covers topics in transportation, the human body, technology and manufacturing, communication, energy and environment, and space and defense. *For a description of exhibits, see p95.*

Shedd Aquarium★★★

1200 S. Lake Shore Dr. 312-559-0200. www.shedd.org. Open Mon–Fri 9am–5pm. Sat–Sun 9am–6pm. Closed Dec 25. All-access pass: $28.95 adults, $19.95 children (ages 3–11). Admission is discounted for Chicago residents.

Hard by Lake Michigan, the Shedd Aquarium brings the ocean to the lakefront. As the world's largest indoor aquarium, it houses aquatic creatures from around the globe—from tiny, jewel-like spiny lobsters to 1,500-pound beluga whales. The Shedd's exhibits and programs emphasize conservation and the environment, and its remarkable animals bring the message vividly to life. The building opened in 1930 and resembles a monument to the Roman sea god, Neptune, whose trident tops the roof. Inside, keep an eye out for

Caribbean Reef, John G. Shedd Aquarium

© Shedd Aquarium/Brenna Hernandez

MUSEUMS

49

Best of the Beasts

Of course you won't want to miss the dolphins, whales, and sharks, but don't overlook some of the less obvious aquatic wonders at the Shedd. Our favorites include **Nickel** the Lucky Sea Turtle, who lives in the Caribbean Reef tank. You'll know her by her "limp," a reminder of injuries from which she is recovering. The name? During her rehab, vets found a nickel lodged in her throat. And be sure to pay your respects to Granddad, the 80-year-old lungfish which arrived at the aquarium as a youngster in 1933. Oh, and those green things you see in many habitats? They're heads of romaine lettuce—a favorite treat among certain residents.

decorative wave and shell patterns and charming sea creatures that crawl over light fixtures, tiles, and doorways. A pioneer at re-creating aquatic habitats, the Shedd has transformed many of its older exhibits into mini-ecosystems that support not only fish but plants, birds, and a furry surprise or two.

Dive In!

When you buy your admission ticket, you'll receive a schedule of feedings, demonstrations, and shows for that day.

Oceanarium★★ – This amazing habitat re-creates a Pacific Northwest ecosystem. Stroll

No Silly Animal Tricks

Shedd animal behaviorists are adamant about the motive behind the Marine Mammal Presentations. The behaviors you'll see reflect natural activities in the wild. A spy-hopping dolphin, for instance, stands straight up on its tail for a better view above the water. The animals are also taught certain behaviors to make medical exams easier. *Oceanarium shows are held daily 10:30am, 11:30am, 1:30pm & 3:30pm; with an extra 4:30pm show on weekends.*

"along the coast," following the edge of the oversized pools where beluga whales, Pacific white-sided dolphins, and harbor seals carouse. The wide expanse of Lake Michigan stretches beyond, a vista barely interrupted by the oceanarium's glass wall. Beneath the pools, underwater viewing galleries bring you nose to snout with graceful dolphins. And be prepared to laugh at the penguin habitat, where beguiling rockhoppers, magellenics, and gentoos go about their business, diving, swimming, and waddling.

Wild Reef★★ – This extraordinary exhibit takes you deep into a Philippine coral reef to see one of the world's most diverse habitats. Displays explain the life cycle of the reef and illustrate how living corals form, survive, and die.
A huge wall of water teeming with gemlike fish against a backdrop of artificial coral bends around the space. See sharks up close and personal in the impressive tank around the corner, and watch underfoot to see little stingrays darting and gliding. So as not to harvest coral from the wild, the Shedd grows (or fabricates) its own. Wild Reef offers excellent narrated dives at 10:30am.

Dolphins jumping, Shedd Aquarium

©Shedd Aquarium/Brenna Hernandez

Amazon Rising: Seasons of the River★ – In these galleries you'll experience a year in the life of an Amazon floodplain forest. Habitats are stocked with some 250 species, including a huge anaconda and a tiny pigmy marmoset.

Caribbean Reef★ – If you stare long enough into these 90,000 gallons of fishy fun, you might spot all of the 500 tropical fish that live there, including hammerhead sharks, rays, and a sea turtle named Nickel *(see box, opposite page)*. Stick around for feeding time, which happens five times a day.

Adler Planetarium★★

1300 S. Lake shore Dr. 312-922-7827. www.adlerplanetarium.org. Open daily 10am–4pm, third Thur every month 6–10pm. Closed Thanksgiving Day & Dec 25. $27 adults, $21 children (ages 3–11); fee includes admission, Atwood Experience, and two sky shows.

It's worth the **views**★★ up and down the lakefront to walk out to the Adler, which occupies a beautiful setting. The oldest planetarium in the Western Hemisphere, it is also renowned for its fine collection of historic astronomical instruments and its splendid sky shows.

Museum Campus Eats

You have plenty of choices for lunch at Museum Campus visit. Enjoy fresh sandwiches (or take a coffee break) in the shadow of Sue the T-rex at the Field Museum's **Corner Bakery**. (If the kids vote for **McDonald's**, you'll find it in the basement.) Visit the **Bubble Net Food Court** at the Shedd Aquarium for pizza, burgers, and the like. For the only table service on the Museum Campus, try **Soundings Restaurant** at the Shedd Aquarium. The menu features gourmet sandwiches, soups—and, yes, seafood—wine and cocktails in an attractive dining room overlooking the lake *(if you wish to dine but not visit the aquarium, reservations are required: 312-692-3277)*. **Galileo Café** at the Adler Planetarium offers cafeteria-style sandwiches, salads, and soups as well as a stunning view. Or bring your own picnic supplies and dine *al fresco* on the campus grounds in summer.

Chicago's planetarium sprang from philanthropist Max Adler's belief that a Zeiss projector (used for re-creating the night sky on an enclosed dome) would be a great teaching tool for the city. He donated $1 million, and architect Ernest A. Grunsfeld Jr. designed a compact, red-granite jewel for the dramatic setting at the tip of Northerly Island. A major renovation in 1999 added 60,000 square feet of exhibit space that enclosed two-thirds of the old Art Deco building in glass. As you make your way through the new space, note the charming bronze signs of the zodiac that still adorn each corner of the original 12-sided structure.

The Sky's the Limit
StarRider® Theater★★ – Located on the lower level, "the world's first interactive computer-graphics theater" immerses you in the stars on its domed screen. Here you'll voyage through the universe, land on Mars, or visit the tombs and temples of ancient Egypt.

History of Astronomy Gallery★ – *Lower level*. This gallery showcases the planetarium's extensive collection of curious historic instruments for measuring time, earth, and space, including the first Chicago planetarium, the 1913 **Atwood Sphere**.
If more modern space exploration suits your taste, visit **CyberSpace**, where news about the latest Mars landings and space-probe discoveries are broadcast at VisionStations. The Adler hosts many topical events throughout the year. Check schedules for special lectures and educational sessions.

Adler Planetarium

© City of Chicago/GRC

University of Chicago★★

From 55th St. on the north to 60th St. on the south, between Dorchester & Maryland Aves. The main quad lies along 58th St., between Ellis & University Aves. This handsome 190-acre urban campus is steeped in history, reputation, and, well, Nobel Prizes (78 have been awarded to students, researchers, and faculty—more than any other school). Founded in 1890 with a strong academic vision, the U of C blossomed early into one of the nation's leading research schools. In the early 1940s, the abandoned football grandstands concealed the Manhattan Project laboratory of Enrico Fermi, whose team of physicists achieved the first self-sustaining nuclear reaction. Immerse yourself in collegiate atmosphere with lunch at **Medici** *(1327 E. 57th St.; 773-667-7394)*, where students have gathered to eat pizza and burgers for decades.

Oriental Institute★★

1155 E. 58th St., at University Ave., on the University of Chicago campus. 773-702-9514. www.oi.uchicago.edu. Open year-round Tue–Sat 10am–6pm (Wed until 8:30pm), Sun noon–6pm. Closed major holidays.

Oriental Institute

©Oriental Institute, University of Chicago

While the institute is dedicated to the study of languages, history, and cultures of the ancient Near East, its museum contains one of the world's choicest collections of Near Eastern art and antiquities. Most of its 75,000 artifacts were collected by institute archeologists, including James Henry Breasted, who in 1904 led the University of Chicago's first field expedition to the land we now know as Iraq, and who created the institute in 1919.

The institute has resided in its current building on the University of Chicago campus since 1931. The museum galleries underwent extensive renovation and now proceed from Prehistory through **Mesopotamian, Assyrian, Egyptian, Persian, and Nubian** galleries with temporary exhibits at the end. The massive 16-foot-tall human-headed winged bull deom Assyrian King Sargon II's Khorsabad is a highlight.

Don't miss the gift shop, which sells better-than-average museum shop fare, including quality jewelry.

Lunch at Big Shoulders

312-587-7766. Light and healthy lunches (including children's specials) compete with great views of Lincoln Park in this café, set in a two-story glass-enclosed turret at the Chicago History Museum. Notice the re-creation of the massive archway framing the inside doorway; it once marked the entrance to the Union Stockyards, site of Chicago's infamous slaughterhouses in the 19C.

MUSEUMS

Puck's

On the east side of the Museum of Contemporary Art. Overlooking the sculpture garden and Lake Michigan beyond an expansive glass wall, Puck's features fine dining with a view. The menu highlights Wolfgang Puck's signature Chinois chicken salad and a selection of specialty pizzas along with salads and sandwiches *(reservations recommended; 312-397-4034; www.mcachicago.org).*

Chicago History Museum★

1601 N. Clark St., at North Ave. 312-642-4600. www.chicagohs. org. Open year-round Mon–Sat 9:30am–4:30pm (Thu until 8pm), Sun noon–5pm. Closed Jan 1, Thanksgiving Day & Dec 25. $14 with audio tours (ages 12 and under free). Free Mon.

Don't miss a visit to the Chicago History Museum, located at the southwestern corner of Lincoln Park. Organized in 1856, the city's oldest cultural institution covers America until 1865 and Chicago since the first explorers. Its collections are chock-full of documents and objects connected to Chicago's first settlers, as well as historic photographs, memorabilia from Chicago's two world's fairs, and, of course, the Chicago Fire.

Chicago History Museum

© City of Chicago/GRC

Museum of Contemporary Art★

220 E. Chicago Ave. 312-280-2660. www.mcachicago.org. Open year-round Wed–Sun 10am–5pm (Tue until 8pm). Closed Jan 1, Thanksgiving Day & Dec 25. $10 (ages 12 and under free). Free Tue.

The task of presenting the avant-garde can be daunting, but the MCA does a good job of making the works and movements of the art of our time accessible to everyone through thoughtful label writing, audio programming, and free guided tours *(check schedule at desk)*. Exhibits mounted on a rotating basis from the museum's 7,000-piece permanent collection generally occupy the third- and fourth-floor galleries.

Much of what you'll see focuses on new acquisitions and works by living artists, but the museum's collection also includes the art of Marcel Duchamp, Max Ernst, René Magritte, Alexander Calder, Andy Warhol, and a host of Chicago and Illinois artists such as Ed Paschke, June Leaf, and Jim Nutt.

The MCA staff are excellent event planners. If you are traveling with kids, find out if you'll be in town during Family Day, periodic Saturdays when the whole family (including the dog) is welcome for free, hands-on programming.

MUST SEE

Installation view of the Smart Museum of Art's gallery of contemporary art, featuring works by Art Green, Christina Ramberg, Sarah Canright, Karl Wirsum, Suellen Rocca, Ed Paschke, and Roger Brown

©Tom Van Eynde/Smart Museum of Art

Smart Museum of Art★

5550 S. Greenwood Ave., on the University of Chicago campus. 773-702-0200. www.smartmuseum. uchicago.edu. Open Tue–Fri 10am–4pm, Thu 10am–8pm, weekends 11am–5pm. Galleries closed Mon and major holidays.

Opened in 1974 and named for the founders of *Esquire* magazine, this small jewel of a university museum holds 7,500 pieces spanning 5,000 years. The Smart Museum rotates its permanent collection, which excels in arts of the late 19C and early 20C century, among four major galleries. Highlights include the Robie House dining room set by Frank Lloyd Wright, an impressive collection of Asian art including scroll paintings, European works dating to antiquity and featuring Renaissance and Baroque paintings, and contemporary work. The Elden sculpture garden occupies the courtyard between the Smart Museum and adjacent Art History building and boasts works by Louise Nevelson, Richard Hunt, Scott Burton, Jene Highstein, and Amando Pomodoro.

Dining with the Prairie School

Tucked away in Lincoln Park, just a short way north of the nature museum, sits a romantic little restaurant **North Pond** *(2610 N. Cannon Dr.; 773-477-5845; www.northpondrestaurant.com)*. Once a skaters' warming hut on the edge of North Pond, the building still serves as a cozy retreat from winter's chill, as well as a cool oasis in summer. Beautifully renovated in Prairie style with warm oak, copper, and art-glass accents, the space now houses an elegant eatery that features local and regional ingredients and wines from small American vineyards. Tall windows look out over the pond, the park, and the city skyline, and a fieldstone fireplace completes the ambience. Be sure to reserve a table in the front room if you wish to dine with the best view and near a roaring fire in winter.

MUSEUMS

Chinese-American Museum of Chicago

238 W. 23rd St. 312-949-1000. www.ccamuseum.org. Open Fri 9:30am–1:30pm. Sat–Sun 10am–5pm. $2 adults, $1 children.

This relatively new museum in Chinatown features a rotating schedule of temporary exhibits, illuminating the Chinese-American experience, particularly in the Midwest. Previous exhibits have included Chinese immigration and the Great Lakes, toys and games and leisure activities of Chinese-American immigrants. In addition to its exhibition space, the museum hosts lecture and other community events throughout the year and is an excellent resource for those wanting to do research on the Midwestern Chinese-American experience.

DuSable Museum of African American History

740 E. 56th Pl. 773-947-0600. www.dusablemuseum.org. Open Mon–Sat 10am–5pm, Sun noon–5pm. Closed Mon Jun–Dec, Jan 1, Thanksgiving Day & Dec 25. $10 adults, $7 students and seniors. Chicago residents $8. Free Sun.

Founded in 1961 by Dr. Margaret Goss Burroughs in her home, this cultural and historical museum now occupies a former park administration building. The modern Harold Washington Wing, added to the structure's south side in 1992, houses cultural programs that supplement permanent and traveling exhibits on African-American life, art, and history.

There is also a Community Gallery where artists can exhibit works related to the subjects of the museum.

International Museum of Surgical Science

1524 N. Lake Shore Dr. 312-642-6502. www.imss.org. Open May–Sept, Tue–Sun 10am–4pm, Oct–Apr, Tue–Sat 10am–4pm. $10 adults, $6 students and seniors. Separate fee for special exhibits. Free on Tue.

Not for the art snob, the International Museum of Surgical Science offers quirky fun for the curious in the Gold Coast. This 1917 French chateau-style building has four floors, jam-packed with all manner of medical miracles. Check out the ephemera of both Eastern and Western healing practices, ranging from weird-looking apparatus (including an iron lung) and instruments to fine art about medicine, not to mention details about all kinds of odd illnesses. The Hall of Murals is just as its name suggests: a room devoted to the topic at hand created by Italian painter Gregorio Calvi di Bergolo (1904–94). While the museum takes a fairly erudite approach to its mission, the collections are still not for those made queasy by science.

Intuit: The Center for Intuitive and Outsider Art

756 N. Milwaukee Ave., 312-243-9088, www.art.org. Open Tue–Sat 11am–5pm, Thu 11am–7:30pm. $5, children under 12 free.

Chicago has countless lesser-known gems, many of which overshadow the Sears Tower in terms of cultural experience. But of all the overlooked cultural institutions, perhaps the most significant is Intuit, the country's leading institution to highlight unschooled folk art, housed just north of downtown.

Officially, Intuit defines its brand of "intuitive and outsider art" as the "work of artists who demonstrate little influence from the mainstream art world and who seem instead motivated by their unique personal visions." Outsider art can also be called "art brut," non-traditional folk art, self-taught art, and visionary art. The museum's permanent collection includes works by Henry Darger, perhaps the best known of all the outside artists. Darger worked as a janitor in Chicago, and his drawings and paintings only brought him fame after his death in 1973.

Intuit is now home to many of the drawings, books, and furnishings from his one-room apartment. Other artists in the collection include sculptor James "Son" Thomas, and sharecropper's son S.L. Jones. Temporary exhibitions and special events continue the efforts to educate the world on self-taught artists.

No matter what, don't skip the museum's sculpture garden.

Leather Archives and Museum

6418 N. Greenview Ave. 773-761-9200. www.leather archives.org. Open Thu, Fri noon–8pm, Sat–Sun noon–5pm. $10.

Strictly for grown-ups! For those who are curious, and not traveling with kids, these two buildings can entertain and inform. The museum collection includes shirts, posters, banners, and other accouterments of the leather fetish and sadomasochism world. The collection includes some of the largest assembly of original Etienne works, photos, sexual devices, and other related materials. There is also a research library for those whose interest in the sexually charged topic is more academic.

Mitchell Museum of the American Indian

3001 Central St., Evanston. 847-475-1030. www.mitchell museum.org. Open Tue–Sat 10am–5pm (Thu until 8pm), Sun noon–4pm. $5 adults, $2.50 children, $10 for a family.

This extraordinarily kid-friendly museum is the only one in the area dedicated to the Native American experience. Its collection includes artifacts and artworks that are part of Native American history, but also are put of the community today. Works cover from the Paleo-Indian period to modern day, and tribes from the North American Indian and Inuit people. The museum hosts ongoing hands-on events and exhibits, so kids (and grown-ups) can make headdresses, learn Native American dance, and see how the traditions of the indigenous community is still part of Midwestern culture today.

Dia de los Muertos

Day of the Dead (celebrated from October 31 to November 2) is a time of great festivity in Mexico, and it's a lot of fun at the National Museum of Mexican Art, too. A blend of ancient Aztec and Christian rituals, including feasting, parades, and the building of colorful home altars, the holiday honors the spirits of those who have died. Women bake skeleton-shaped bread, and children crave *calaveras*, grinning candy skulls. Families visit and decorate cemeteries, singing and dancing as a way of scorning death. The museum celebrates the season annually with demonstrations, programs, and an exhibition of Day of the Dead crafts—incorporating symbols such as skulls, skeletons, and marigolds.

Museum of Contemporary Photography

600 N. Michigan Ave. 312-663-5554. www.mocp.org. Open Mon–Sat 10am–5pm, Thu 10am–8pm, Sun noon–5pm. Free.

Housed on the campus of Columbia College Chicago, this photography museum is more than a mere academic effort. With more than 8,500 photographs in its permanent collection, MoCP is the place to go in the Midwest to see the work of the best American photographers since 1936. Highlights of the collection include the works of Ansel Adams, Diane Arbus, and Jim Dine. The Midwest Photographers Project is a rotating collection that is on loan to the museum for two years. In addition to the artworks, the museum has lightboxes and sculpture.

Museum of Holography

1134 W. Washington Blvd. 312-226-1007. Open Wed–Sun 12:30–5pm. $5 adults, children under 12 $4, children under 6 free.

This quirky museum seems tiny in comparison to the art institutes of the world. And, in our digital age, holography is not the mind-bender it used to be. But this West Loop institution packs a lot into its small space, so there is more than you can imagine. The holographs here are sophisticated and likely to change any preconceived notions about the technology. Also exhibited is information on holographs used for the medical profession.

National American Italian Sports Hall of Fame

1431 W. Taylor St. 312-226-5566. www.niashf.org. Open Mon–Fri 9am–5pm, Sat–Sun 11am–4pm.

Nestled in Little Italy (where else?), the hall honors the athletes of Italian descent, a surprisingly varied group. In the first-floor Tommy and Jo Lasorda Exhibit Gallery you'll find mementos including Mario Andretti's Indy 500 racecar, Rocky Marciano's World Heavyweight Championship belt, and Vince Lombardi's last coat worn as coach of the Green Bay Packers. The artifacts are accompanied by video and audio clips. Don't miss the sculpture of Joe DiMaggio in the pretty plaza across the street.

National Museum of Mexican Art

*1852 W. 19th St. 312-738-1503.
www.nationalmuseumofmexican
art.org. Open year-round Tue–Sun
10am–5pm (Wed until 8pm).
Closed major holidays.*

The largest institution of its kind in the US, this respected ethnic center is best known for its exhibits and programs focusing on Mexico's colorful celebration of the Day of the Dead *(see box, left)*. A 33,000-square-foot addition enables the museum to exhibit works from its permanent collection in **Mexicanidad: Our Past Is Present**, which journeys from prehistory to the present. Note the stunning beaded mural called *New Awakening*. Temporary exhibits feature a wide range of Mexican artists, indigenous cultural expressions, and community activism, notably the mural movement so evident in the Pilsen neighborhood. More recent installations examine the contemporary topic of immigration through different art exhibits, lectures, and other programs.

Peggy Notebaert Nature Museum★

*2430 N. Cannon Dr.
773-755-5100. www.nature
museum.org. Open year-round
Mon–Fri 9am–4:30pm, Sat–Sun
10am–5pm. Closed Jan 1,
Thanksgiving Day & Dec 25. $9
adults, $6 children (ages 3–12).
Free Thu.*

Beautifully sited on Lincoln Park, along the lower end of North Pond, this sand-colored "cluster of wedge-shaped blocks" was

designed to resemble the sand dunes that once covered this area. Opened in 1999, the museum aims to help visitors "think green" through environmental learning and an appreciation of our dwindling natural resources. Inside, six permanent exhibits fill two levels; outside, pathways wind through native plantings.

Butterfly Haven★ – The air on the second floor is aflutter with 70 species of butterflies, many so beautiful you may mistake them for flowers. Watch out: one of the residents might just hitch a ride on your shoulder! Check out the chrysalis case and talk to the interpreter. If a chrysalis is hatching while you're visiting, you'll be spellbound by the process.

Wilderness Walk – Ants and other live bugs and creatures, along with walk-through dioramas, help you to picture the sand dunes, prairies, and savannas native to the greater Chicago area.

Nature's Lunchbox - Learn about the food cycle from farm to table to compost.

RiverWorks – To get the lowdown on the Chicago River and other similar waterways, visit this first-floor exhibit, where you—and the kids—can splash around and create dams, locks, runoffs, and even sewers.

Extreme Green House – See a full-sized bungalow in the middle of the museum, with live animals and hands-on kiosks designed to illustrate how we are connected to the environment.

Polish Museum of America

984 N. Milwaukee Ave, 773-384-3352. www.polishmuseumof america.org. Open Fri–Wed 11am –4pm. $7 adults, $6 seniors and students.

The Polish immigrant population is one of Chicago's largest and most proud. This neighborhood museum, in the heart of what was once the epicenter of the local Polish community, is a look at the Polish-American museum. On display are artworks by Polish artists, folk art and costumes, and space is devoted to that icon of Polish descent: the late Pope John Paul II.
The second-floor **Paderewski Room** has an excellent display of memorabilia of the Polish composer and statesman Ignacy Jan Paderewski.
Highlights of the **Great Hall** include a massive stained-glass window, memorabilia of Shakespearean actress Helena Modjeska, and the restored **Leszczynski sled**, carved from a single piece of oak.

Smith Museum of Stained-Glass Windows

On Navy Pier, 600 E. Grand Ave. at Lake Michigan. 312-595-5024. Open year-round Mon–Thu 10am– 8pm, Fri & Sat 10am–10pm, Sun 10am–7pm.

Filling a series of galleries along the lower-level terraces of Festival Hall, this unique museum showcases more than 100 stained-glass windows from 1897 to the present, all works of art in themselves. Their creators include well-known names such as Louis Comfort Tiffany and John LaFarge, as well as Chicago artists Ed Paschke and Roger Brown.

Spertus Museum

610 S. Michigan Ave. 312-322-1700. www.spertus.edu/museum. Open Sun–Thu 10am–5pm, free admission to basic exhibits.

Housed at the Spertus Institute of Jewish Studies, the museum expanded thanks to the new Spertus building which opened in late 2007. Housed on three floors, the museum has more than 15,000 pieces of Jewish ephemera on display, along with topical permanent and traveling exhibitions relating to Jewish themes. Spertus is known for its thought-provoking public programs. The new facility is home to a terrific gift shop.

McCormick Tribune Bridgehouse and Chicago River Museum

See p76. 376 N. Michigan Ave.

Richard H. Driehaus Museum

See p77. 40 E. Erie St.

Swedish-American Museum and Children's Museum of Immigration

See pp101, 104. 5211 N. Clark St.

PARKS AND GARDENS

Urbs in Horto, **City in a Garden, has long been Chicago's nickname, and you'll see why when you experience the city's parks and gardens—old, new, and renewed. Park District gardeners plant over 550,000 annuals and perennials and 156,000 bulbs each year, along with 8,000 trees and shrubs. As a result, sweeping green spaces, pocket parks, and even the medians and parkways of major thoroughfares such as Lake Shore Drive blossom with color.**

Millennium Park★★★

Bounded by Michigan Ave., Randolph & Monroe Sts and Columbus Dr. Open year-round daily 6am–11pm. 312-742-1168. www.millenniumpark.org.

Mayor Richard J. Daley's "park du triomphe" opened In the summer of 2004 to boisterous acclaim from critics and public alike. In spite of some grumbling about the gargantuan ($475 million!) price tag, most everyone agrees that the park is indeed a triumph. By day or night (it's beautifully illuminated in the evenings), this is no ordinary park. Though not one for pets (dogs are forbidden), the park's 24.5 acres beckon at every turn with something to see, touch, or experience. Crowded with delights, Millennium Park offers an escape from the daily grind. And it serves another more practical purpose by masking an unsightly area of railroad tracks and parking lots that now operate below the park's well-manicured surface.

Best of the Millennium

Jay Pritzker Pavilion★★★ – Above all, literally, hovers the metallic mayhem of architect Frank Gehry's proscenium arch that marks this state-of-the-art outdoor theater. Sails, clouds, a cherry bomb in a soda can— everyone has an opinion about Gehry's oversized scramble of stainless steel, and you will too. The theater accommodates 4,000 in fixed seats and 7,000 on the oval-shaped fairway, which is covered with a trellis that holds speakers up and out of the

©Steve Geer/iStockphoto.com

BP Bridge, Millennium Park

© Anne Evans/Chicago Architecture Foundation

Cloud Gate (2004-06) by Anish Kapoor, Millennium Park, Chicago

way. This "waterproof" lawn is specially designed to drain away rainwater in 15 minutes. Gehry's 120-foot overhanging "headdress" shelters the stage itself, which is lined with pine wood. It's even air-conditioned for the comfort of the **Grant Park Orchestra and Chorus** *(312-742-7638; www. grantparkmusicfesitval.com)*, which holds free concerts at the Pavilion throughout the summer.

Cloud Gate★★★ – Affectionately known as the Bean, this sculpture by Anish Kapoor has become the surprise favorite of the park. The gleaming structure of stainless steel—66 feet long, 33 feet high, and weighing 110 tons—draws visitors like moths to a flame. Its jelly-bean shape creates fantastic reflections of the city skyline and the crowds—go ahead, walk up and pick yourself out. Better yet, step under the Bean and gaze up into its shiny underbelly. The effect is a kind of cross between a city gate, a majestic rotunda ceiling, and a carnival mirror.

BP Bridge★★ – Getting there is all the fun on this meandering bridge designed by Frank Gehry.

Crown Fountain

© City of Chicago/GRC

In 925 feet of luxurious serpentine curves, the bridge connects Millennium and Grant parks over Columbus Drive. It's clad in stainless-steel panels that enclose walkers without the need for handrails. The broad hardwood deck slopes gently, inviting you to pause and take in the cityscape from every angle. Kids love to run the length of it (though this is frowned upon). The bridge also buffers the Pritzker Pavilion from traffic noise.

Crown Fountain★★ – For something completely different, check out the Crown Fountain, where huge projected faces spit water out of their mouths like modern gargoyles. The two 50-foot towers of steel, glass, light, and water are the work of Spanish artist Jaume Plensa, and they don't sound nearly as pleasing as they are in person. Best of all, a shallow, black-granite reflecting pool between the towers proves wonderful for wading and splashing, as kids quickly discover. Watch carefully as the faces (a total of 300, soon to be 1,000), all Chicagoans, change slowly over the course of several minutes.

© City of Chicago/GRC

Lurie Garden★ – This planted sanctuary is truly a work in progress since the perennials will take a year or two to fill in and the protective pine hedgerow, known as the Shoulder Hedge, requires about ten years to mature. From the hedge, the garden slopes gently to the south to maximize its sun. A wooden boardwalk and watery pools, called the Seam, bisect the planted spaces.

Grant Park★★

Bounded by Roosevelt Rd. & Randolph St. on the north and south, and Michigan Ave. & Lake Shore Dr. on the west. 312-742-7648. www.chicagoparkdistrict.com.

Overshadowed by its glitzy neighbor Millennium Park, Grant Park remains dignified and beautiful in an old-fashioned way. The city's 319-acre "front yard" marks roughly the midpoint in the swath of parks that trims Chicago's 28-mile lakeshore. The park has been shaped by landfill, accretion, erosion, and the human hand since 1830 when state commissioners set aside a thin strip of land along the shoreline to "remain

Grant Park

Fests, Feasts, and Fun in Grant Park

In the summer months, Grant Park is *the* place to be for Chicagoans and visitors. Topping the list of special events is **Taste of Chicago**, which attracts more than three million people over ten days to sample local eats (skip this festival on July 3 and 4 unless you enjoy a mob). No admission fee is charged, but food vendors only take tickets. Purchase tickets with cash or credit at any of several booths.

Grant Park also hosts Chicago's renowned music festivals, all held at the **Petrillo Bandshell** and featuring headline entertainment free of charge:

Chicago Blues Festival, 1st weekend in June

Chicago Gospel Festival, June

Chicago Country Music Festival, during the Taste of Chicago

Chicago Jazz Festival, Labor Day Weekend

forever open, clear and free." Sixty years later, mail-order magnate A. Montgomery Ward conducted a lengthy and successful battle with the city to clear the stables, railroad tracks, and other eyesores that had rooted there in spite of the old edict. In 1909 architect Daniel Burnham drew up a comprehensive plan for the city of Chicago, calling for a "formal focal point," and the elegant landscaping of the park began to emerge as construction started in 1915. Though the automobile age sliced up the green space with busy streets, the park still offers peaceful gardens, picnic spots, and lovely vistas of the city and lake. Tennis courts and a playground occupy the park's shady northeast corner.

Fact: History was made on November 5, 2008 in Grant Park, where Barack Obama was announced President Elect of America.

What's What in Grant Park

Museum Campus★★★ –
The southern part of the park is home to the city's popular triad of museums: **Field Museum of Natural History**★★★, **Shedd Aquarium**★★★, and **Adler Planetarium**★★ *(see p51)*.

Buckingham Fountain★★
Columbus Dr. at Congress Pkwy.
Centerpiece of Grant Park, the

Buckingham Fountain

© City of Chicago/GRC

Clarence Buckingham Memorial Fountain is truly a lakefront jewel. Donated to the city by philanthropist Kate Sturges Buckingham to honor her brother, the fountain was completed in 1927 at a cost of $750,000. A $2.8 million restoration, completed in April 1995, returned the fountain to its original splendor. It's modeled on a fountain at the Palace of Versailles in France, but is nearly twice as large. Intended to represent Lake Michigan, the fountain pumps 1.5 million gallons from the lake, recirculating all but what's lost through spray and evaporation—stand downwind on a hot, windy day for a refreshing spritz. Three basins of Georgia pink marble rise from the main pool; gargantuan carvings of seaweed and shells encircle the outside of each basin. In the large pool, four bronze sea horses, each 20 feet long, represent the states that border the lake.

If you become enamored of the Fountain (and really, who doesn't?), consider donating to the Parkways Foundation's $25 million restoration project. Some parts of the fountain have not been upgraded since 1927, and many cold Chicago winters have wreaked havoc on the marble structure. See www.restorethefountain.com for more information.

A Fountain of Facts
- Buckingham Fountain is among the largest fountains in the world.
- At its maximum, the center jet shoots up 150 feet.
- The bottom pool measures 280 feet across, the lower basin is 103 feet, the middle basin is

Water and Light
As spectacular as the fountain's monumental scale are the water-and-light shows that flow from the basin during the summer. The fountain's 134 jets pump water at a rate of 14,100 gallons a minute and the central jet shoots water skyward to create a dazzling effect *(May–Oct dusk–11pm; 312-747-2474)*. Once controlled entirely by hand, the choreography of water and light is now regulated by computer.

60 feet, and the upper basin is 24 feet.
- 820 lights color the fountain's water and light display.

Lincoln Park★★

Visitor Center: Lincoln Park Cultural Center, 2045 N. Lincoln Park West. 312-742-7726. www.chicagopark district.com. Open year-round Mon –Fri 9am–9pm, Sat 8am–4pm, Sun 10am–3pm.

Except for the occasional stray bone, it's hard to tell that this was once a soggy cemetery. Today the sweeping expanse is one of Chicago's most compelling landscapes. Unlike so many urban areas with waterfronts blighted by industry, Chicago provides unlimited access to the lake via its numerous lakefront parks. Among

Touring Tip

To enjoy Lincoln Park, start at the **Standing Lincoln** between LaSalle Street and North Avenue and wend your way north to Diversey Parkway.

Café Brauer

2021 N. Stockton Dr. Open year-round daily 11am–5pm. 312-742-2400.
This café makes a good stopping point on your walk through the park for a fresh brew or a bite to eat. In summer you can enjoy the beer garden overlooking South Pond. Architect Dwight Perkins, whose other credits include some of the animal houses at Lincoln Park Zoo, designed this refectory in 1908 for restaurateurs Paul and Caspar Brauer. A striking example of the Prairie School style, it hugs the pond with its main pavilion and flanking loggias. Arts and Crafts details—chandeliers, tiles, mosaics, and windows—lend the interior a suitably rustic charm.

the finest is Lincoln Park. The cemetery was established here in 1837, but as the city limits bulged northward from downtown, the cemetery's new neighbors lobbied for replacing it with parkland. Moving the corpses took time, but by the 1880s the heart of the park was well established. Filling in the land over the next decades extended the park to its northern limits by 1957. Today stretching six miles and 1,200 acres along the shoreline of Lake Michigan, from Oak Street north to Ardmore Avenue, Lincoln Park trims the city's watery edge with a pleasant and peaceful greenbelt. At North Avenue, the park forms the northern edge of the affluent **Gold Coast★** *(see p32)*, and, at Clark Street, the eastern boundary of

the lively **Lincoln Park/DePaul★** neighborhood, where theaters, restaurants, and shops abound and the streets of the **Old Town** and **Mid-North** historic districts offer insights into 19C architecture and daily life.

A Walk in the Park

Lincoln Park Zoo★★ – *See p99.*
2200 N. Cannon Dr.

Peggy Notebaert Nature Museum★ – *See p59. 2430 N. Cannon Dr.*

Alfred Caldwell Lily Pool★ – *Enter from the north off Fullerton Pkwy.*

Step into this secret garden and enter another world. Originally planned in the Victorian style in the

Lincoln Park

1880s, the garden was reshaped as a wooded grove in 1937 by landscape architect Alfred Caldwell. The plot spent much of its life as the zoo's Rookery until Caldwell's Prairie-style vision was restored in 2002. Today this tranquil enclave is a haven for birds and bird-watchers alike.

Lincoln Park Conservatory –
2391 N. Stockton Dr. 312-742-7736.
Open year-round daily 9am–5pm.
Modeled in 1892 on London's Crystal Palace, the glass and copper structure and its 15 propagating houses, greenhouses, and gardens now cover three acres.

Garfield Park Conservatory★

300 N. Central Park Ave.,
in Garfield Park. 312-746-5100.
www.garfieldconservatory.org.
Open year-round daily 9am–5pm,
Thu 9am–8pm.

Built in 1908 by landscape architect Jens Jensen, Garfield Park Conservatory has become popular for exhibits that integrate sculpture or objects (such as dinosaur skeletons) into the foliage.

Look for the work that glass artist **Dale Chihuly** left in the Aroid House after his big show here in 2001. The conservatory mounts several shows a year, as well as market days on summer weekends. Restoration of the conservatory has created stunning results; the newly renovated **Palm House**, for example, contains 3,500 plants.

PARKS AND GARDENS

© City of Chicago/GRC

Garfield Park Conservatory

World's Columbian Exposition

In a battle to host the 1893 World's Columbian Exposition, Chicago earned its enduring nickname "Windy City" because of all the blustery boasting that led to its winning the honor over other cities. Conceived to celebrate the 400th anniversary of Columbus' discovery of America, this world fair covered 650 acres along present-day Jackson Park and encompassed 200 buildings erected by leading architects. From opening day on May 1, 1893 through October, the exposition awed 27 million visitors with its architecture and attractions, including the world's first Ferris wheel and the infamous "Little Egypt" dancing the hootchie kootchie. Floodlights illuminated the Neoclassical buildings, creating a sparkling white, fairy-like atmosphere. But the fair was fleeting as its construction was built entirely of "staff," a temporary material left to crumble away at the event's end.

Jackson Park

E. 56th to 57th Sts., Stony Island Ave. to Lake Michigan. www.chicagoparkdistrict.com.

Located eight miles south of the Loop along Lake Michigan's shoreline, the park's 600 acres of playing fields, lagoons, and lush vegetation began as a wasteland of sand dunes and scrub marshes. Famed landscape architect Frederick Law Olmsted (designer of Central Park in New York City) first laid out the park in 1870. He later redesigned and completed it for the World's Columbian Exposition in 1893, creating a series of lagoons and formal ponds as its centerpiece. In addition to the features that remain from the fair, Jackson Park features an 18-hole golf course.

Fragments of the fair include **Columbia Basin★**, a reflecting pool designed by Olmsted for the Palace of Fine Arts, now the **Museum of Science and Industry★★★; Osaka Gardens★**, at the north end of the sanctuary on Wooded Island; and **The Republic★**, the 24-foot-high "Golden Lady" cast by Daniel Chester French—the only sculpture in the park.

Osaka Gardens, Jackson Park

© City of Chicago/GRC

GREATER CHICAGO

0 — 3 mi
0 — 6 km

GLENCOE, LAKE FOREST \ Chicago Botanic Garden★★

WILMETTE
★★NORTH SHORE
Baha'i House of Worship★★
Northwestern University
SKOKIE
EVANSTON
Rogers Park
Lifeline Theatre
Devon Ave.
Rosehill Cemetery★
UPTOWN
Wilson Skatepark
Puppet Parlor
Graceland Cemetery★★
Lincoln Park★★
★Wrigley Field
★LINCOLN PARK/ DEPAUL
Bailiwick Rep. Theater
Athenaeum Theatre
Apollo Theater
★Peggy Notebaert Nature Museum
Humboldt Park
Vittum Theater
★Garfield Park Conservatory
Garfield Park
United Center
MAGNIFICENT MILE★★★
THE LOOP★★★
NEAR WEST SIDE
National Museum of Mexican Art ■
CHINATOWN
BRIDGEPORT CANARYVILLE
PILSEN
U.S. Cellular Field
BRONZEVILLE
Burnham Skatepark
Burnham Park
NEAR SOUTH SIDE
HYDE PARK KENWOOD
★David and Alfred Smart Museum of Art
★★Robie House
★★★MUSEUM OF SCIENCE AND INDUSTRY
DuSable Museum of African-American History★★
UNIVERSITY OF CHICAGO
Jackson Park
63rd St. Beach
Oriental Institute★★
South Shore
Oak Woods Cemetery
EVERGREEN PARK
★PULLMAN HISTORIC DISTRICT

LAKE MICHIGAN
ILLINOIS INDIANA

O'HARE AIRPORT
MIDWAY AIRPORT
★★Brookfield Zoo | Morton Arboretum★
★Illinois & Michigan Canal NHS |

Hotels
1. City Suites Hotel
2. Hawthorne Terrace
3. The Homestead
4. Hotel Orrington
5. Majestic Hotel
6. The Willows Hotel
7. Wooded Isle Suites

Restaurants
1. Andies
2. Ann Sather
3. Aruns
4. Club Lucky
5. Davis Street Fishmarket
6. Erwin
7. Green Zebra
8. Half Shell
9. Heaven on Seven
10. Hema's Kitchen
11. Revolution Brewing
12. Tapas Barcelona
● Trio Atelier

PARKS AND GARDENS

HISTORIC SITES

Chicago's fascinating history takes in industry and robber barons, immigrants and labor movements, and, of course, architecture. Here are some of our favorite sites from the city's past.

Graceland Cemetery★★

4001 N. Clark St., Lakeview. From downtown, take Lake Shore Dr. north and turn left on Irving Park Rd. to the cemetery. 773-525-1105. www.graceland cemetery.org. Open year-round daily 8am–4:30pm. Closed Dec 25, July 4 & Labor Day.

Graceland Cemetery

© Steve Geer/iStockphoto.com

For a slice of Chicago history, check out this cemetery, just north of Wrigley Field, where notable architecture and sculpture mark the resting places of many of the city's movers and shakers. Developed in 1860, Graceland received many of the corpses that were exhumed from the lakeshore cemetery where construction of Lincoln Park was under way. Stroll the 119-acre grounds yourself (pick up a site plan at the entrance) or check with the Chicago Architecture Foundation about its next Graceland tour. And no, Elvis is not buried here, but you will find monuments to Chicago industrialists, politicians, and architects set amidst ponds and a rolling landscape.

Notable Residents

Be sure to pay a visit to the tombs of Henry Harrison Getty and Martin Ryerson (both designed by Louis Sullivan), Marshall Field (designed by Daniel Chester French), Potter and Bertha Palmer, Daniel Burnham, Peter Schoenhofen, and George Pullman *(see p74)*, all in the northern half of the cemetery. To the south rest boxing great Jack Johnson and National League

More Local Haunts

If Graceland shelters the remains of Chicago's historic elite, the lovely **Rosehill** *(5800 N. Ravenswood Ave.; 773-561-5940)* hosts local merchants, bankers, and businessmen who made this the City that Works. Many of Chicago's mayors rest here, along with Civil War generals and soldiers. Founded in 1859, Rosehill is Chicago's largest cemetery. If the Gothic entryway looks familiar, it's because it replicates the **Water Tower and Pumping Station★** downtown *(see p42)*. On the city's South Side, **Oak Woods Cemetery** *(1035 E. 67th St.; 773-288-3800)* is even older (1854), and lodges some of the city's most interesting residents: Mayor Harold Washington, Chicago's first African-American mayor; Olympian Jesse Owens; activist Ida B. Wells; and physicist Enrico Fermi. *For more about local cemeteries, visit www.graveyards.com.*

MUST SEE

Can't Get Enough Frank Lloyd Wright?

Calling all FLW fans. You've been to Robie House *(see below)*. You've been to Oak Park *(see p78)*. But wait, there's more. A handful of Wright's residential architecture (all privately owned) still stands in Chicago, much of it on the South Side:

Adams House (1900–01)	9326 S. Pleasant Ave.
American System-Built Houses (1917)	10410 and 10541 S. Hoyne Ave.
Bach House (1915)	7415 N. Sheridan Rd.
Foster House and Stable (1900)	12147 S. Harvard Ave.
Heller House (1897)	5132 S. Woodlawn Ave.
Roloson Houses (1894)	3213–19 S. Calumet Ave.
Waller Apartments (1895)	2840–48 W. Walnut St.
Walser House (1903)	42 N. Central Ave.

founder William Hulbert, who is spending eternity under a large baseball.

Robie House★★

5757 S. Woodlawn Ave., on the University of Chicago campus. Take Lake Shore Dr. south to 53rd St. and turn left on Woodlawn Ave. 708-848-1976. www.gowright. org. Visit by one-hour guided tour only, year-round Mon–Fri 11am, 1pm & 3pm, weekends every 20min 11am–3:30pm. Closed Jan 1, Thanksgiving Day & Dec 25. $9. By bus, take #6 Jackson Park Express to Stony Island Ave. &

57th St.; walk west 6 blocks to Woodlawn Ave. and go left one block.

This home made its designer, **Frank Lloyd Wright**, world famous and helped "break the box" of traditional architecture. In 1908, wealthy inventor Frederick Robie commissioned architect Wright to design his residence in Hyde Park. The resulting home, with its distinctive horizontal lines, is considered a masterpiece of modern architecture.

The Robies lived here only for a year or so, after which time the

©University of Chicago

Robie House

house passed through a number of different owners. It was saved from the wrecking ball at the 11th hour in 1957 and is now operated by the University of Chicago in conjunction with the Frank Lloyd Wright Home and Studio Foundation, which is supervising an intensive ten-year restoration. Inside, the hallmarks of the Prairie style are all here: the long, low horizontal lines, side-hingeing casement windows, the hidden front entrance, built-in furniture, and the grand hearth that separates living from dining space. Stained, leaded and art-glass windows are done in geometric patterns, and Wright's trademark globe-shaped "moonlight" ceiling fixtures provide lighting. Note the long Roman bricks that Wright favored, which accentuate the horizontal even more.

Hutchinson Street District★

Between Lake Shore Dr. & Hazel St. www.cityofchicago.org/Land marks/H/HutchinsonStreet.html.

Several designs by Prairie School architect George Washington Maher, together with a range of eclectic, single-family homes, provide a welcome diversion from the high-rise lakefront landscape in the Lakeview neighborhood. The **Edwin J. Mosser House** (1902), at no. 750, features oversized urns and a Sullivan-esque entrance facing Clarendon Street. At no. 817, the two-story **Claude Seymour House** (1913) is distinguished by leaded-glass windows, urns, and a wide, overhanging roofline, and Maher's signature flattened-arch entrance. Maher's **Grace Brackenbush House** (no. 839) marks the integration of picturesque period revival elements with the horizontal emphasis of the Prairie School. The 1894 **John C. Scales House** (no. 840) is a Queen Anne home replete with shingles and round turrets.

Jane Addams Hull-House Museum★

800 S. Halsted St., on the University of Illinois campus. From the Loop, drive west on W. Adams St. and turn south on Halsted St. 312-413-5353. www.uic.edu/jaddams/hull. Open Tue–Fri 10am–4pm, Sun noon–4pm. Closed major holidays.

Hull House not only captures but reimagines and re-creates the

Jane Addams Hull-House Museum

©Vince Michael/Michelin

history of immigration and social activism in Chicago. Founded in 1889 by pioneering social workers Jane Addams and Ellen Gates Starr, the settlement house became a focal point for citywide and national movements to improve living and working conditions of the urban poor and disadvantaged. Observing similar work in London (England) in 1886, 26-year-old Addams returned to Chicago inspired. In 1889 she and Starr moved into a Near West Side neighborhood teeming with immigrant families (the house they occupied was built in 1856 by real-estate developer Charles Hull). With like-minded resident activists, they pursued an aggressive agenda of education, social justice, and workplace reform, and Hull House grew to a complex of 13 buildings—including Chicago's first public gymnasium, art and music schools, and a cooperative residence for working women. Today only the house and the Residents' Dining Hall remain, energized by a 2010 renovation that displays Jane Addams' bedroom and details other activists' achievements. Visitors are invited to participate in the same issues a century later through soup kitchens, video, sound and interactive installations that set the standard for 21C house museums.

While You're in the Neighborhood . . .

Around the corner from Glessner House, the **National Vietnam Veterans Art Museum** exhibits a powerful collection of works by veterans of the war in Southeast Asia (*1801 S. Indiana Ave.; 312-326-0270; www.nvvam.org; not recommended for children*). Once the Chess Records Studio, famous for recording Muddy Waters, Howlin' Wolf, Chuck Berry, and other blues greats, **Blues Heaven** (*2120 S. Michigan Ave; 312-808-1286; www.bluesheaven.com*) now houses a foundation created to document the blues and to support blues artists (*studio tours Mon–Fri noon–3pm, Sat noon–2pm*).

HISTORIC SITES

Prairie Avenue Historic District★

Drive south from the Loop on Michigan Ave., turn left at 18th St. and continue two blocks to Prairie Ave. (no through traffic). www.cityofchicago.org/Landmarks /P/PrairieAveDistrict.html.

The area south of downtown is among the hippest, fastest-growing residential section of the city. But this modern phenomenon recalls how Prairie Avenue grew after the Chicago Fire in 1871. Here on "Millionaire's Row" lived industrial and commercial leaders Marshall Field and George Pullman, among others, in mansions designed by famous architects such as Richard Morris Hunt, Burnham & Root, and Henry Hobson Richardson.

For a while, Prairie Avenue was the city's most fashionable address, but families moved to the North Side as industry invaded the neighborhood after 1900. In contrast, State Street between 16th and 22nd streets became the notorious Levee, an area of saloons and brothels. By 1966 industrial growth had caused the demolition of most of Prairie Avenue's mansions; a Chicago Landmark District was created in 1979 to preserve the remaining homes.

House Museums

Two of the city's most historically significant house museums form the district's core. One-hour tours of either or both *(312-326-1480)* begin at the coach house of Glessner House. Neighborhood tours are offered on alternating Sundays from July to September.

John Jacob Glessner House★★

1800 S. Prairie Ave. www.glessner house.org. Tours Wed–Sun 1pm & 3pm. $10 ($15 for both houses), $6 ages 5–12. Wednesdays free. Closed major holidays.

Designed by H.H. Richardson in 1886, the Glessner House revolutionized domestic American architecture with its open floor plan and plain facade. John Glessner, a manufacturer of farm implements, commissioned the house at a time when labor unrest alarmed the city's wealthy residents. In response, the architect designed the mansion like a fortress by turning its back to the street and including a secure inner courtyard.

Henry B. Clarke House★

1855 S. Indiana Ave. 312–326–1480. www.clarkhousemuseum.org. Tours Wed–Sun noon & 2pm. $10. $6 ages 5–12. Wednesdays free. Closed major holidays.

Built in 1836 for New York merchant Henry Clarke in the Greek Revival

Library, Glessner House Museum

Courtesy of Glessner House Museum

MUST SEE

Pullman is located about 13 miles south of the Loop. To get there by car, drive south on I-94 and exit at 111th Street westbound (Exit 66A). The Pullman Historic District is four blocks west of the expressway. To get there by train, take the Metra Electric District Line from the Randolph Street Metra Station; exit at 111th Street *(fare and schedule information: 312-836-7000; www.metrarail.com).* Begin your visit at the **Historic Pullman Foundation Visitor Center** *(11141 S. Cottage Grove Ave., entrance on 112th St. side; open year-round Tue–Sun 11am– 2pm; closed major holidays),* which features a video presentation and exhibits, and stocks maps and brochures. Guided walking tours depart from the visitor center on the first Sunday of the month *(May–Oct 1:30–3:30pm).*

style (notice the heavy columns on the front porch), this white clapboard home is considered Chicago's oldest structure. It was moved here in 1977 from South Wabash Avenue.

Pullman Historic District★

Between 107th & 115th Sts. along Cottage Grove Ave. 773-785-8901. www.pullmanil.org.

Located in an industrial district on the Far South Side, this fascinating community was created by railroad-car magnate **George Pullman**—famous for his luxurious train coaches—in 1881 as an experimental company town. He incorporated the Pullman Palace Car Company in 1867, but ten years later striking rail workers shocked the nation and open conflict between labor and management threatened.

Wishing to isolate his employees from the strike- and strife-prone city, Pullman built his new factory town on 500 acres 13 miles south of Chicago. He hired architect Solon Beman and landscaper Nathan F. Barrett to design the factories and a comprehensive town plan. Pullman ran his "perfect

town" for a profit, maintaining ownership of all the property in the community, collecting rents from workers and refusing to let anyone own individual houses. But economic depression in the 1890s brought wage cuts, and to keep the town profitable, Pullman raised rents and food prices. The company's employees rebelled, and strikes and bloody conflict led to the end of Pullman's plan. In 1971 the town was listed on the National Register of Historic Places; its restoration continues today.

Pullman Historic District

©Vince Michael/Michelin

HISTORIC SITES

Hotel Florence

© Vince Michael/Michelin

A Walk Through the District

After years of neglect, the community was lovingly restored and today is best sampled by a stroll down the 19C streets. A variety of Victorian residences fill the 16 blocks of the South Pullman residential district. The larger homes of managers face 111th Street, while smaller row houses and double houses of craftsmen and workers line the streets south to 115th Street. Varied and picturesque rooflines are typical of the Queen Anne style so popular among Victorian architects

(but more often seen on larger houses). Architect Solon Beman also designed the simpler homes of North Pullman *(between 104th & 108th Sts)* for workers of two other factories; the most charming stretch of houses are staggered along Cottage Grove Avenue at 107th Street. Most homes are private residences, so you will be looking at exteriors only, but a number of historic homes are open the second weekend in October for the **Annual Pullman House Tour** *(11am–5pm; call 773-785-8901 for tickets)*. Closed for restoration, you can still see the exterior of the **Hotel Florence** *(1111 S. Forestville Ave.)*—named for Pullman's daughter—which was off-limits to workers and where only visiting businessmen could drink.

Rest in Peace

Pullman's social experiment did not end well, and employees turned on him in anger when he lowered wages but refused to lower rents. When he died in 1897, his family was so worried that his grave in Graceland Cemetery would be robbed that they covered the coffin in tar paper and asphalt, sealing it into a concrete block. Railroad ties were used to overlay and safeguard the tomb further. As far as we know, the sleeping-car prince still rests securely in peace.

McCormick Tribune Bridgehouse and Chicago River Museum

376 N. Michigan Ave. 312-977-0227. www.bridgehousemuseum.org. Open May–Oct, Thu–Mon 10am–5pm. Admission to the museum is $4 adults, $3 seniors and students, age 5 and under free.

It has been almost 40 years since this bridge tower, the southwest tower of the Michigan Avenue Bridge, was used for bridge tenders. While striking on the outside, it was all but forgotten on the inside. The non-profit Friends of the Chicago River raised funds to lease the historic space from the city of Chicago, and turned it into a museum that illustrated how the city grew up on the river. Exhibits include information on the river and ecology, the role the river played in the city's founding, and the city's many bridges.

Check the schedule to try to visit during one of the 100 times annually when the bridge is lifted to accommodate sailboats. It is a feat of engineering.

The exterior of the tower, which is visible even when the museum is not open, features bas-reliefs of important moments in the city's history, sculpted by J.E. Fraser and Henry Hering in 1928.

Richard H. Driehaus Museum

40 E. Erie St. 312-932-8665. www.driehausmuseum.org. $25 adults, $15 children ages 12–16. Public tours Tue, Wed & Sun at 10am, 1pm & 3 pm. Children under the age of 12 are not permitted in the museum.

Nestled in the recently renovated former mansion of Samuel M. Nickerson is the city's newest museum. Built between 1879 and 1883, Nickerson's Marble Palace was one of the prime examples of the Gilded Age in Chicago, built in a Classical style and possibly one of the most expensive homes ever built in Chicago.

Richard H. Driehaus, a well-known Chicago businessman, bought the mansion in 2003 and spent five years bringing it back to its Marble Palace-era glory—part of his ongoing attempt to get Chicagoans to appreciate and protect Neoclassicism as much as they do modern architecture. Along with original furnishings, the mansion now houses Driehaus' collection of fine and decorative arts, including Tiffany lamps and windows, and other opulent decorative items of eras gone by.

Stephen A. Douglas Tomb and Memorial

636 E. 35th St. 312-225-2620. www.illinoishistory.gov/hs/doug las_tomb.htm. Wed–Sun, call for hours. Free.

US Sen. Stephen A. Douglas (1813–61) is best known for his performance in his debates against Abraham Lincoln. His gravesite sports a 96-foot-tall tower, the top of which can be seen from Lake Shore Drive. Most locals just drive past, but exiting the Drive is worthwhile. The mausoleum contains four bronze allegorical figures representing Illinois, history, justice, and eloquence.

In addition to the tomb, the Bronzeville site has well-manicured gardens and grass, providing a surprising, serene state park nestled in a busy, urban neighborhood. A few blocks west on 35th Street visit the exhibits and learn about the Black Metropolis community at the **Bronzeville Visitors Information Center** *3501 S. M.L. King Drive, 773-373-2852, Mon–Fri 10am–5pm, Sat 10am–6pm. Free.*

EXCURSIONS

Need a break from bustling downtown? A jaunt beyond the city limits reveals different worlds in any direction. Beaches and dunes lie south and east, history to the southwest, beautiful trees and great architecture to the west, and lovely gardens to the north. So take your pick!

Frank Lloyd Wright Home and Studio

Oak Park★★★

10mi west of Chicago via I-290 West to Harlem Ave. exit. Turn right on Harlem Ave. and proceed north. Visitor information: 708-524-7800 or 888-625-7275; www.visitoak park.com. See map p81.

What do the modern house, *For Whom the Bell Tolls*, and Tarzan have in common? Oak Park, of course! Perhaps best known for its enclave of homes designed by architect **Frank Lloyd Wright** *(see box, p79)*, Oak Park is also the birthplace of Ernest Hemingway and the one-time home of Edgar Rice Burroughs, creator of Tarzan. Founded after the Great Chicago Fire in 1871 by a prosperous

Touring Tip

Visiting Oak Park: If you arrive by car, the Lake Street parking garage *(between Kenilworth & Forest Aves.)* is most central to the attractions. To get there by public transportation, take the CTA Green or Blue Line, or take the Metra West commuter rail from the Metra station at W. Madison and Canal Sts. Exit all train lines at Oak Park Ave. or Harlem Ave. *(312-836-7000. www.metrarail.com).* You can catch the Oak Park Shuttle at train stations around town *(daily 10am–5:30pm; 708-343-4830).* **The Oak Park Visitors Center** *(158 N. Forest Ave.; 888-625-7275; www.visitoakpark.com; open year-round daily 10am–5pm; closed Jan 1, Thanksgiving Day & Dec 25)* is a good place to pick up maps and guides, buy attraction tickets, and rent a guided audio tour for your walk around the neighborhood *($10).*

MUST SEE

Frank Lloyd Wright

Frank Lloyd Wright's best-known works revolutionized residential building design. Born in Wisconsin in 1867, Wright came early under the influence of renowned architect Louis Sullivan, apprenticing in Sullivan's studio until striking out on his own at age 25. Living and working in Oak Park, he developed his distinctive Prairie style, its strong horizontal lines and overhanging eaves inspired by the flat midwestern landscape. Inside, Wright flowed rooms one into another and he designed furniture to complement his organic designs. In a scandal that effectively ended his practice in socially conservative Oak Park, Wright left his wife and six children in 1909. Wright remained in the limelight until his death in 1959 at age 91. His total number of designs exceeds 1,100, nearly half of which were actually built.

Puritan population, the little suburb grew rapidly. Today Oak Park is economically stable and socially progressive, accommodating various lifestyles with relative ease. Its shady, tree-lined streets, historic attractions, upscale boutiques, and cozy restaurants make the suburb a must-see destination, especially for architecture buffs.

Frank Lloyd Wright Home and Studio★★

951 Chicago Ave. 708-848-1976. www.wrightplus.org. Visit by 45min guided tours only, year-round Mon–Fri 11am, 1pm & 3pm; weekends 11am–3:30pm. Closed Jan 1, Thanksgiving Day & Dec 25. $12.

Wright first built this house in 1889 and continued to remodel and add to it over time; his alterations reveal his architectural growth. Restored to its 1909 appearance, when Wright last lived there, the original structure features the horizontal bands of windows and low profile of the Prairie style. Notice the cozy inglenook in the living room and the signature furnishings, all designed by Wright.

Unity Temple★★

875 W. Lake St. 708-383-8873. www.unitytemple-utrf.org. Open Dec–Feb daily 1–4pm. Rest of the year Mon–Fri 10:30am–4:30pm, weekends 1–4pm. Guided tours weekends 1pm, 2pm & 3pm. Pre-arranged, customized tours are available by calling 708-383-8873. Closed Jan 1, Thanksgiving Day & Dec 25.

Wright called this Unitarian temple "my jewel," and it's easy to see why. The interior features a deceptively simple design that is both intimate and awe-inspiring, and remarkably bright considering the heavy concrete exterior. This, the only major public building from Wright's Prairie period, celebrated its centenary in 2008.

Forest Avenue★

Walk south from Wright's home and studio to see a wonderful cross section of his residential work (pick up information at the visitor center). Begin by wandering west on Chicago Avenue. Numbers 1019, 1027, and 1031 are "bootleg" homes that the 25-year-old architect designed in violation of his exclusive contract with Adler & Sullivan in 1892–93.

EXCURSIONS

The 1902 **Frank W. Thomas House**★ at no. 10 is considered Wright's first true Prairie-style house; it abandons all the fuss of Victorian design that you see in the row houses just south.

The Rest of Oak Park's Best

"Pleasant Home"★
217 S. Home Ave. 708-383-2654. www.oprf.com/phf. Visit by one-hour guided tour only, Thu–Sun Mar–Nov 12:30pm, 1:30pm & 2:30pm. Dec–Feb 12:30pm & 1:30pm. Closed major holidays. $10.

Here's a Prairie-style home designed by another architect, George Washington Maher (1864–1926), whose work can be seen throughout the suburbs of Chicago. He designed the 30-room "Pleasant Home" (aka Farson-Mills House) in 1897 for banker John Farson.

"Pleasant Home"

© Darris Lee Harris/Pleasant Home Foundation

Ernest Hemingway Birthplace
339 N. Oak Park Ave. 708-848-2222. www.hemingway.org. Visit by guided tour only, year-round Sun–Fri 1–5pm, Sat 10am–5pm. $10.

This restored Victorian home built in 1890 re-creates the comfortable family upbringing of celebrated author Ernest Hemingway (1899–1961). A visit here also provides a glimpse of Oak Park's social order in the early 20C and the impact that the community had on the author's early development. Admission includes the Hemingway Museum two blocks south *(200 N. Oak Park Ave.; same hours & contact information as Birthplace)*, focusing on the first 20 years of the writer's life.

North Shore★★
31mi from downtown Chicago to Lake Forest. Follow Lake Shore Dr. / Sheridan Rd. north.

Chicago's northern suburbs collectively conjure up a vision of elegant living called the North Shore. The lovely—and unusual—geography of ravines, bluffs, beaches, and woodlands, and the area's architecture and history combine to make a drive up the shore an enjoyable one-day excursion. Take your time and stop for lunch, take a peek around a village center, or enjoy one of the many beaches along the way. (During summer, some townships charge nonresidents for beach or park admission.)

Brookfield Zoo★★
See p97. 8400 W. 31st St.

Chicago	Ave.		1031 1027 1019	**★★Frank Lloyd Wright** **Home & Studio**		Chicago	Ave.
River			Moore House	Heurtley House		Superior	St.
Oak	St.		Hills-DeCaro House	Elizabeth Ct.		**Ernest Hemingway Birthplace**	
Pl.	**Forest**			Gale House		Erie	St.
Quick	Ave.		Austin Gardens Park	**Thomas House★**		**Hemingway Museum**	
Pl. Brae		Marion		Ontario		St.	
Holly Ct.		Forest Ave.	Cummings Square	**★★★OAK**	Scoville Park	**PARK**	
Clinton	Lake	Harlem	**Oak Park Visitors Center**	St.	**★★Unity Temple**	Lake	St.
Bonnie		HARLEM/ LAKE		North			Blvd.
Central Ave.						OAK-PARK	
Circle Ave.		South	Blvd.		Ave. St.	Ave.	Ave.
Franklin	St.		**★"Pleasant Home"**	Pleasant St.		Ave.	Ave.
Forest		Maple	Mills Park	Home Ave.	Kenilworth	Grove	Oak Park
Dixon	St.	Marion					Euclid
Park			Randolph	St.			Linden

Hotels
1 The Carleton of Oak Park
2 The Write Inn

Restaurants
1 Avenue Ale House
2 Café le Coq

Getting To Know the North Shore

Baha'í House of Worship★★
100 Linden Ave., Wilmette.
847-853-2300. www.us.bahai.
org/how. Open year-round daily
7am–6:30pm; visitor center open
year-round daily 10am–5pm.
Guided tours Sun 1:45pm.
The lacy, opalescent dome of the Baha'í temple will startle you as you cross from Evanston to Wilmette on Sheridan Road. The mammoth, nine-sided structure, rising 191 feet, cuts an exotic profile against the low suburban skyline. This is the North American seat of the Baha'í faith, whose members follow the teachings of the 19C Persian prophet Baha'u'llah, believing in the "oneness" of religion and of humankind. Why is the only North American temple located here? The

religion was introduced at the 1893 World's Columbian Exposition held in Chicago. Construction of the temple, which began in 1909, took nearly 50 years to complete.

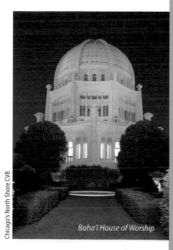

Chicago's North Shore CVB

Baha'í House of Worship

EXCURSIONS

81

North Shore Rest Stops

Downtown Evanston and Central Street a little farther north both teem with restaurants and shops. In Wilmette, try **Convito Italiano** *(1515 Sheridan Rd., in Plaza del Lago; 847-251-0123; www.convitoitaliano.com)* for a delightful trattoria lunch or dinner, or the makings of a gourmet picnic from its market. Tiny **Ravinia Bistro** *(581 Roger Williams Ave., Highland Park; 847-432-1033)* serves French country fare and delectable pastries. Along Sheridan Road in Highwood, you'll find a gaggle of notable French and Italian restaurants. When you reach Lake Forest, stop by **Market Square★** *(700 N. Western Ave.)*, a village shopping and dining center since the early 1900s.

Chicago Botanic Garden★★

1000 Lake Cook Rd., Glencoe. 25mi north of Chicago via I-90/94 West to I-94 and US-41. Exit at Lake Cook Rd. and go east .5mi. 847-835-5440. www.chicago-botanic.org. Open year-round daily 8am–dusk. Closed Dec 25. Parking $20/car.

With 26 garden areas, more than a million individual plants of 7,000 different varieties, and a host of birdlife, the 385-acre preserve makes a lovely stop at any time of year. The heart of the garden occupies the largest of nine islands in a 60-acre artificial lagoon. Begin at the **Gateway Visitor Center**, and consider a tram tour *(late Apr–Oct daily 10am–3:30pm;*

Chicago Botanic Garden

$5) for a narrated overview. Highlights include the formal **Rose Garden★**, the six "rooms" of the **English Walled Garden★**, the tactile and fragrant **Sensory Garden**, and the **Japanese Garden★**, called Sansho-En ("the garden of three islands"). In summer, kids will enjoy the **Model Railroad Garden**, 7,500 square feet of miniature American landscapes crisscrossed by 15 model train lines *(open daily 10am–5pm; $3)*. You can have a sit-down lunch or a snack here, too, in the **Garden Café**, the outdoor **Grille**, or the **Rose Terrace Café**.

Morton Arboretum★

4100 Rte. 53, Lisle. 25mi west of downtown via I-290 West to I-88 tollway West; exit on Rte. 53 and go north. 630-968-0074. www.morton arb.org. Open Apr–Oct daily 7am–7pm (or sunset, depending which is earlier). Rest of the year daily 7am–5pm. Gatehouse fees: $11, $8 children (2–17). Wednesdays $7.

Joy Morton used the fortune he made at the helm of Morton Salt Company to establish this arboretum on 400 acres in 1922. Today sprawling over 1,700 acres, the outdoor museum is both a serious scientific laboratory

Chicago's North Shore CVB

MUST SEE

of woody plants from around the world and a lovely place to spend the day. You'll find oaks, elms, lindens, sugar maples, and 3,300 other tree and plant types organized into family groups, landscape groups, geographic groups, and habitat groups. Whether you choose to hike the 14 miles of trails, drive the nine-mile circuit or spend the day exploring the 36,000-square-foot **visitor center** and surrounding gardens, you're in for a treat. There is also a Children's Garden to keep the little ones amused *(Apr–Oct 9:30am–5pm, Nov–Feb 9:30am–4pm, until 6:30pm Thu May–Sept)*.

Mitchell Museum of the American Indian
See p57. *3001 Central St., Evanston.*

Illinois & Michigan Canal National Heritage Corridor★

Southwest of Chicago via I-55 south to Rtes. 45 & 171. Visitor information: Heritage Corridor Convention and Visitors Bureau, 800-926-2262 or www.heritage corridorcvb.com; and the Canal Corridor Association, 815-588-1100 or www.canalcor.org.

Running 96 miles from Bridgeport to LaSalle/Peru, the Illinois & Michigan (I&M) Canal first linked the Great Lakes to the Mississippi River in 1848 and helped Chicago build its reputation as an industrial powerhouse. Until 1882 when steamboats took over, mules pulled barges laden with lumber, stone, and grains through 15 locks that equalized the 160-foot difference in water level between the canal in Chicago and the Illinois River.

Best Ways to Experience the National Heritage Corridor

The scenic 61-mile **I&M Canal State Trail★** runs along the old towpath from Rockdale to LaSalle *(access at Channahon, Exit 248 from I-55)* and provides a historic route you can hike, bike, or snowmobile. At LaSalle, where the canal and Heritage Corridor end, you'll find **Lock no. 14★**, the only lock that is completely restored *(Canal Rd., off Rte. 351)*.

Touring Tip

During good weather, enjoy the full sweep of the arboretum on the **Acorn Express**, a narrated, one-hour, open-air tram tour *(departs from the visitor center year-round; 630-968-0074; $5)*.

By 1914, the new Sanitary and Ship Canal replaced the northern section, and in 1933 the Illinois River was made navigable in the southern reaches.
Now long obsolete, the canal is preserved in a **National Heritage Corridor** and a series of parks, trails, and preserves. The waterway passes through suburbs and industrial areas, as well as the historic canal towns of **Lemont**, **Lockport★**, **Joliet★**, **Morris**, **Seneca**, **Marseilles**, **Ottawa★**, **Utica**, and **LaSalle**, some more ravaged than burnished by time.

Lockport★

15mi southwest of Chicago via I-55 south to LaGrange Rd./Rte. 45 (Exit 279A).

As the location of Lock no. 1 and the old Canal Commission

Fine Dining on the Prairie

One of the region's finest restaurants occupies a restored 1895 building in Lockport's historic district. **Tallgrass** *(1006 S. State St.; 815-838-5566)* offers contemporary French cuisine in prix-fixe menus of three, four, or five courses. For lunch, or a less pricey dinner, choose **Public Landing** *(815-838-6500)*, located in the Gaylord Building. Farther down the pike, enjoy lunch or dinner in the rustic supper-club atmosphere at **Starved Rock Lodge** *(Rtes. 178 & 71; 800-868-7625; www.starvedrocklodge.com)*.

Lockport

headquarters, Lockport once bustled with the comings and goings of barges, canallers, merchants, wagons, and mules. Old grain warehouses—the Gaylord and the Norton buildings—bookend the historic district, which encompasses the blocks between the canal and 7th, Washington, and 11th streets. Restored to its 1860s appearance, the **Gaylord Building★** *(200 W. 8th St.; 815-*

588-1100; www.gaylordbuilding. org; open year-round Tue–Sat 11am–5pm, Sun noon–5pm) is a National Trust historic site with an information desk and exhibits that explore the history of the canal and its impact on Illinois. To the south, the 1850 **Norton Building** now houses the **Lockport Gallery**, which exhibits the work of past and present Illinois artists *(201 W. 10th St.; 815-838-7400; www.museum. state.il.us/ismsites/lockport/; open year-round Mon–Fri 9am–5pm, Sun noon–5pm; closed major holidays)*. In between the Gaylord and Norton buildings, the **Lincoln Landing★** features a 2009 sculpture by David Ostro commemorating the 16th president's connection to the canal. The **I&M Canal Museum** is located in the original Canal Commission headquarters *(803 South State St.;*

Gaylord Building

Reddick Mansion
© Donna Nordstrom/Reddick Mansion Association

815-838-5080; visit by guided tour only, year-round daily 1–4:30pm). From there, walk through Lockport's beautiful downtown historic district, which extends three blocks along State Street (Route 171), or follow the 2.5-mile **Gaylord Donnelley Canal Trail★** from the Gaylord or Norton buildings for a look at the massive limestone walls of Lock no. 1. West of the canal extends the lovely, 269-acre **Lockport Prairie Nature Preserve★** *(Rte. 53 & Division St.; 815-727-8700; www.fpdwc.org/lockport.cfm; open Apr–Oct daily 8am–8pm; rest of the year daily 8am–5pm).*

Ottawa★

79mi southwest of Chicago via I-55 south to Rte. 23 (Exit 90).

This town was built on glass. Silica sand from its famous quarries was shipped to and fro on the canal, and by 1900 the city was a leading glass producer.

In **Washington Park**, senatorial candidates Abraham Lincoln and Stephen A. Douglas held the first of their famous 1858 debates. Douglas was a frequent guest at the 1856 **Reddick Mansion★**, adjacent to the park *(100 W. Lafayette St.; 815-433-6100; www.cityofottawa.org/reddick. htm; open year-round Mon–Fri 9am–5pm, Sat 9am–4pm, Sun 10am–2pm).* The Reddick Mansion can be toured *(telephone to book)* and is also hired as a venue for meetings, weddings, wedding receptions, and other events.

Indiana Dunes National Lakeshore★

40mi south of Chicago via I-94/ I-90 to I-90; exit at US-20/US-12. Follow US-12 to the lakeshore sites. Visitor information: 219-926-7561; www.nps.gov/indu.

Indiana Dunes State Park

1600 North 25 East, Chesterton, Indiana. 219-926-1952. www.state.in.us/dnr/park lake/parks/indianadunes.html. Open year-round daily 7am–11pm. $8/vehicle ($4/vehicle for Indiana residents). Ensconced within the greater national lakeshore, the state park offers 3 miles of beachfront and 16.5 miles of trails. Amenities here include a bathhouse/pavilion, picnic areas, and a visitor center.

Indiana Dunes National Lakeshore

© Jim West / age fotostock

Looking for a brawnier beach than Chicago offers? Then head south to this 25-mile sliver of pristine land wedged around the heavy industry of northern Indiana. It's about a 40-mile drive, but don't let the intervening smokestacks deter you; the 15,000 acres of windswept beaches, dunes, marshes, and forests of this National Lakeshore are worth the trip. Though brawny they may look, these ancient glacial dunes form a fragile ecosystem at the mercy of prevailing winds, pounding waves, and human encroachment. The effort to preserve them began in 1911 and continues to this day.

Bailly Homestead and Chellberg Farm and Trail★
On Mineral Springs Rd., 6mi east of Inland Marsh. Open 8am–dusk. Though access to these historic buildings is limited to a few occasions a year, a trek around the two-mile trail here reveals a glimpse of early settlement as well as the natural wonders of the dunes.

Mount Baldy★
One of the largest (123 feet) dunes in the park, Mt. Baldy is constantly being pushed inland by the winds, at a rate of 4 to 5 feet a year. The walk up and around the dune to the beach is short *(.5mi)* and very steep. And no, that massive tower you see is not a nuclear plant, but a garden-variety power-plant cooling tower.

West Beach Area★
Turn left on County Line Rd., shortly after entering the park. Open May–Sept daily 9am–9pm. Rest of the year daily 8am–dusk. $6/car mid-May–end of Sept. Pets prohibited. Beware of dangerous undertow. Known primarily for its popular West Beach, this large section of the park also includes Long Lake and 3.5 miles of hiking trails. A walk along the **Dune Succession Trail★** offers a look at the park's surprising biological diversity, encompassing 1,400 plant species.

Barging
Before railroads, canals transported people west and products east. Along with the Erie Canal, the I&M provided an inland link from New York to New Orleans. Up and down the I&M, young canal boys led mules along towpaths pulling 100-foot barges, each loaded with 100 tons of cargo. Today, on the Sanitary and Ship Canal, which runs parallel to the old I&M, one barge can carry 15 times the freight, and tugboats now replace the boys and their mules. To watch a modern lock in operation, stop in Utica at the **Illinois Waterway Visitor Center★** (950 N. 27th Rd.; 815-667-4054; open year-round daily 9am–5pm).

FOR FUN

Residents of "The City of Big Shoulders" may work hard, but they play hard, too. Chicagoans have a great sense of fun, and they love to share it with visitors. What else would you expect from the folks who brought you The Second City *(see p118)*, the Ferris wheel and the Tootsie Roll? So go ahead, have some fun, Chicago style.

Navy Pier★★

600 E. Grand Ave. at Lake Michigan. 312-595-7437. www.navypier.com. Open May–Aug Sun–Thu 10am–10pm, Fri–Sat 10am–midnight. Sept–Oct & Apr Sun–Thu 10am–8pm, Fri–Sat 10am–10pm. Nov–Mar Mon–Thu 10am–8pm, Fri–Sat 10am–10pm, Sun 10am–7pm. Attractions have separate admission fees. Shops & restaurants closed Thanksgiving Day & Dec 25.

Touring Tip

If you do nothing else, take a walk to the end of the 3,000-foot-long pier for some great skyline and lake **views★★**. On summer Saturdays and Wednesdays, fireworks light up the night sky over the pier *(starting at 9:30pm). See p97 for an array of Navy Pier's kid stuff. For information about getting to Navy Pier, see p15.*

Navy Pier has enjoyed many lives since it was first built in 1916 as— you guessed it—a passenger and freight terminal. Then it served as a naval training station during World War II and as a campus for the University of Illinois. It has hosted festivals, conventions, and trade shows. After a period of disuse, the pier was reborn in 1995 as the colorful, bustling, and thoroughly touristy place you see today. Many of Chicago's sightseeing cruise ships come and go from here, giving the place a truly nautical atmosphere.

In its 50 acres, the pier offers something for everyone, from high culture (the excellent Shakespeare Theater; *see p122)* to carnival food and fun. If it's raining, duck indoors to the **IMAX Theater**. Relax amid

Navy Pier

© David Dunai/Apa Publications

FOR FUN

Navy Pier ferris wheel

© David Dunai/Apa Publications

the palms in the tropical **Crystal Gardens** or grab a bite at one of many eateries *(see box, below)*. Outdoors, the 150-foot **Ferris wheel** beckons. **Chicago Children's Museum★** *(On Navy Pier, see p97.)*

Attend a TV or Radio Show Taping

The departure of Oprah Winfrey in 2011 changed Chicago forever, but you can still get tickets to see Jerry Springer's daily show; just plan ahead to join the studio audience, and you must be at least 18 years of age. Tapings generally take place twice on scheduled days during the season.

Jerry Springer Show – *312-321-5365 or www.jerryspringertv.com*. Shows are taped September through April on Monday, Tuesday, and Wednesday, except during weeks of major holidays. You can also get tickets by mail by writing to the studio at 454 N. Columbus Drive, 2nd Floor, Chicago, IL 60611.

For more family-friendly fun, try: – **Wait, Wait Don't Tell Me**, *10 S. Dearborn St. http://chicago publicradio.org. $21.99.* NPR's news quiz is taped in Chicago live most Thursdays. You wouldn't think watching live radio could be this amusing, but it is!.

Gourmet to Grub: Dining at the Pier

Though the fare here is on the touristy side, you'll find a variety of styles and lots of kid-friendly food. Lively **Joe's Be-Bop Café & Jazz Emporium** *(312-595-5299)* serves up southern barbecue and traditional live jazz. **Bubba Gump Shrimp Co. & Market** features, well, shrimp and a lot of artificial "atmosphere" *(312-252-4867; www.bubbagump.com)*. **Charlie's Ale House** offers pub surroundings, complete with 70 beers and a list of single-malt scotches, as well as a family-friendly menu *(312-595-1440)*. For fast food, head to the food court, McDonald's, the beer garden (with free live music), or the **Häagen Dazs Café** for sandwiches and oh-so-rich ice cream. You'll find terrific upscale seafood, steak, and pasta at **Riva**, which also offers more casual dining at its first-level bar *(312-644-7482)*.

Catch a Cubs Game at Wrigley Field

1060 W. Addison St., at Clark St. From downtown, take Lake Shore Dr. north and turn left on Irving Park Rd., then go west on Clark St. 773-404-2827. http://chicago.cubs. mlb.com.

There are a lot of sporting events you could enjoy in Chicago, but there's only one **Wrigley Field★** *(see p43)*. Nestled into a busy residential neighborhood on Chicago's North Side, the field languishes sleepily until baseball season when the joint really starts jumping. Cubs' games sell out quickly, despite the fact that the team hasn't won a World Series in a century. During the season, fans jam neighborhood streets and bars for hours before and after each game. The park seats just over 39,000; seating on the rooftops of neighboring buildings can be reserved for groups *(www.ballparkrooftops.com).* If you can't get into a game, try one of the ballpark tours offered on Saturdays and Sundays during baseball season *(no tours on game days; 773-404-CUBS; http://chicago. cubs.mlb.com; $25).*

Take a Tour of Chicago

Chicago offers a wealth of different tours for every taste. Here's a sampling:

Untouchable Tours – *773-881-1195. www.gangstertour. com. Tours depart from the corner*

Wrigley Field

© David Dunai/Apa Publications

of Clark & Ohio Sts., year-round Mon–Wed 10am, Thu–Sun 10am & 12pm (also 2pm and 7:30pm Fri and 2pm & 4pm Sat). From June 15 Sat 9am, 11am, 1pm, 3pm, 54pm, 7pm, Sun–Fri 10am and 12pm, (also Sun 2pm and 4pm, Wed–Thu 7pm, Fri 7:30pm; $30).

No image of Chicago is more popular, or enduring, than the city as a hotbed of gangsters. Even though Al Capone and his cronies are long gone, you can still tour the notable and notorious landmarks of hoodlumdom, including the site of the St. Valentine's Day massacre, and the **Biograph Theater**, where John Dillinger was shot. Costumed guides conduct these two-hour bus tours in character for a lighthearted look at Prohibition-era Chicago.

Chicago Neighborhood Tours – *312-742-1190. www.chicago neighborhoodtours.com. Tours depart from the Chicago Cultural Center, 77 W. Randolph St. Reservations required. $30 adults; $25 children, includes refreshments.*

One good way to explore some of the Windy City's more than 130 neighborhoods is on a Chicago Neighborhood Tour, offered by the City of Chicago. Visit historic

Bronzeville and the South Side, the soul of Chicago's African-American community, or **Uptown**, home of the city's oldest jazz club. Or discover the ethnic flavors of enclaves like Little Italy, Greektown, or Chinatown. Each tour is offered only a few times a year, so check schedules before you go.

Chicago Architecture Foundation tours – *312-922-3432, caf.architecture.org.* CAF offers a wide range of downtown walking tours, river tours, and neighborhood tours focused on Chicago's rich architectural heritage.

Chicago River Tours – *See p42.*

Ghost Tours – *888-GHOST-91. www.chicagohauntings.com. 600 N. Clark St. $28 adults, $20 children.* See the supernatural side of the city, lead by a local author. The tours include as much history as they do scary stories.

Untouchable Tours

Untouchable Tours

Festival Fun at the Lake

The temperature isn't the only thing that's cooler by Lake Michigan. The annual **4th of July party** (held the evening of July 3) along the downtown lakefront attracts more than a million people. The spectacular fireworks show, set off from barges just outside Monroe Street Harbor, starts at dusk. The city celebrates **Venetian Night** in late July with a parade of illuminated vessels in Monroe Harbor *(8:30pm)*, followed by fireworks over the water set to rock music broadcast on WXRT (93FM). The **Chicago Air and Water Show** attracts 2 million gawkers in August to see the daredevil jet-powered Thunderbirds and acrobatic stunt flyers duck and dodge high-rises at incredible speeds. *For more information, see www.cityofchicago.org/specialevents.*

OUTDOOR FUN

With beaches along Lake Michigan and green spaces galore, Chicago claims plenty of places to play outdoors. So grab your bike, your volleyball, your golf clubs, or your ice skates—whatever the season, you won't run out of things to do.

Outdoor Fun in Millennium Park★★★

Bounded by Michigan Ave., Randolph & Monroe Sts. and Columbus Dr. 312-742-1168. www.millenniumpark.org. Open year-round daily 6am–11pm. See p61.

Arriving by bike? Park it, at no charge, at the **McDonald's Cycle Center** *(Randolph St. & Columbus Drive; 888-245-3929; www.chicago bikestation.com). Free bike parking, $30 monthly pass for secure parking and access to showers and lockers.* During summer festivals and music events, valet bike parking is free! McDonald's Cycle Center also rents bikes by the hour, day, or week, and there's even an on-site repair shop and snack bar. Guided bike/walk tours are offered in spring and fall *(see website).* For wintertime fun in the park, try out those figure-eights at the **McCormick Tribune Ice Rink** *(see p92).*

Oak Street Beach★★

Along the lakefront from 7600 Sheridan Rd., at Howard St., to 9500 E. Ewing Ave., at Calumet Beach. 312-747-0832. www.chicagoparkdistrict.com.

Okay, it's not the Riviera, but Chicago's beaches are sandy, sunny, and beautiful. More than 30 of them line the lakefront from north to south, and lifeguards are on duty from Memorial Day to

Oak Street Beach with Chicago skyline

©City of Chicago/Chris McGuire

Labor Day *(9am–9:30pm).* Some, like the Rogers Park beaches at the north end of the city, are no bigger than a block wide. Others, such as North Avenue Beach and 63rd Street Beach, have bathhouses, concessions, and other amenities, as well as large stretches of sand. Several beaches feature nature trails, others have tennis courts and volleyball set-ups. The best sands to see and be seen? That would be **Oak Street Beach** *(access via tunnels at Oak or Division Sts.),* where the tanned and toned soak up rays and swim in the shadow of the Drake Hotel *(see pp30, 140).*

Park Grill

11 N. Michigan Ave. 312-521-7275. www.theparkgrill.com. For that après-skate dinner, try the rinkside Park Grill, a wood-trimmed, white-tablecloth restaurant serving an upscale American menu. During the summer, the Grill expands into Chicago's largest alfresco-dining venue. You can also reserve picnic bags to go.

OUTDOOR FUN

Lake Michigan can be cold, especially in the spring, but the swimming is pleasant and refreshing. If swimming is restricted because of high bacteria counts in the water, lifeguards will post warning signs.

Ice skating in downtown Chicago

©Jim Jurica/iStockphoto.com

Go Skate

Chicago's long, cold winter has some good points: it sets the scene for some great ice-skating opportunities. The city has nine outdoor rinks *(open late Nov–late Feb)* where you can practice your double axels. Some are listed below *(for a complete list, contact the Chicago Park District: 312-742-7529 or www.chicagoparkdistrict.com).*

◆ **McCormick Tribune Ice Rink at Millennium Park** – *Michigan Ave. between Washington & Madison Sts. 312-742-5222. Open daily 10am–10pm.* Bring your own

blades and skate free of charge, or rent skates *($9).*

◆ **Daley Bicentennial Plaza** – *337 E. Randolph St., in the Loop. 312-742-7650. Open Mon–Fri 10am–3:30pm & 7–9pm, weekends 8:30am–noon. $2 adults, $1 children under age 14. Skate rentals $2 adults, $1 children.*

Gotta grind? Crave a carve? Check out one of Chicago's two permanent street skateparks: 20,000 square feet each of fast concrete fit for old- and new-school skaters alike:

◆ **Wilson Skatepark** – *Wilson Ave. & Lake Shore Dr.*

◆ **Burnham Skatepark** – *31st St. & Lake Shore Dr.*

Hit the Links

Chicago Park District courses: 312-245-0909. www.cpdgolf.com. Open year-round (weather permitting) daily dawn to dusk.

The Chicago Park District has six golf courses, three driving ranges *(open 7am–10pm)*, two miniature-golf courses and three learning centers spread across the city. Daily fees vary from $11 to $25 (slightly higher on weekends) and tee times can be reserved online or by phone. *For a list of courses and details, see www.cpdgolf.com.*

The Green: Putting in Grant Park

Tucked away in an old bus turnaround on Monroe Drive between Lake Shore Drive and Columbus Avenue, this 18-hole putting course *(daily 10am–10pm)* features lush plantings, great views, and downtown convenience.

At par 42, it offers players a chance to practice their short game with a true-golf experience. It's fun for beginners, too. Enjoy lunch, dinner, or a snack at The Green's full-service patio restaurant. Call for reservations and tee times *(352 E. Monroe St.; 312-642-7888; www.thegreenonline.com).*

MUST DO

FOR KIDS

Okay, you've done the architecture, the museums, and the historic sites. Now what about the kids? Or the kid in you? Here are some Chicago spots the whole family can enjoy.

Art Institute of Chicago★★★

111 S. Michigan Ave. 312-443-3600. www.artic.edu/aic. See p44.

Begin your family visit to the AIC in the Modern Wing at the **Ryan Education Center**, where kids are invited to get up close and personal with art, read books, and play hands-on or interactive games in the **Vitale Family Room**, which also hosts family exhibitions. Grab a guide that can make your visit family-friendly. Drop-in workshops and craft programs are offered, and the Institute also fills a calendar with children's events

Touring Tip

To prepare for a visit to the Art Institute with children, check out the museum's website *(above)* for activities and suggestions on how the kids can have fun with art.

that require pre-registration. Make sure you take the kids downstairs in the main building to the **Thorne Miniature Rooms★★**, tiny handcrafted rooms from 68 periods and places around the world. Like fancy dollhouses, each room is furnished on a scale of 1 inch to 1 foot, right down to the rugs and silverware.

Field Museum of Natural History★★★

1400 S. Lake Shore Dr. 312-922-9410. www.fieldmuseum.org. See p46.

Dinos and mummies and bugs, oh my! What more could a kid want? Though much of this museum is geared for older kids and adults, there are some notable highlights for younger visitors—**Sue★★**, the 47-foot-long T-rex, topping the list. For more prehistoric beasts, head to the upper level of the East Wing, where the **DinoZone★★**

Field Museum of Natural History

©The Field Museum

FOR KIDS

Dolphins, Shedd Aquarium

©Shedd Aquarium/Brenna Hernandez

exhibit will delight with skeletons of long-necked *Apatosauruås*, horned *Triceratops*, and the winged *Pteranodon*. On the ground level, **Underground Adventure★** simulates the dark, creepy-crawly world beneath our feet, while the **Crown Family PlayLab** lets young children dress up and become natural scientists. Your young ones may also enjoy **What Is an Animal?** and **Inside Ancient Egypt**.

Shedd Aquarium★★★

1200 S. Lake Shore Dr. 312-559-0200. www.shedd.org. See p49.

This place is a winner with kids of all ages. Brightly colored sea creatures captivate little ones, while bigger kids focus on sharks and piranhas and octopuses. The **Polar Play Zone** lets tots dress up as penguins and slip and slide, ride in a mini-submarine, or touch sea stars. Check out the daily **Animal Encounters** to get up close and personal with tarantulas, turtles, and snakes. The **Tots on Tuesdays** program offers story times, crafts, animal touch programs, music, and characters in costume for preschoolers (ages 3–5). And, of course, neither you nor the kids will want to miss the **Marine Mammal Presentations** in the **Oceanarium★★** or feeding time at the **Caribbean Reef★**.

Hooray for Kayavak!

As you visit the Oceanarium, keep your eyes peeled for Kayavak, a special beluga whale with a white birthmark on her back. The whale's mother died of an infection when Kayavak was only five months old. Because the calf was nursing, this might have meant death for her, too. But keepers at the aquarium were determined to keep Kayavak alive. They weaned her to solid food (fish), hoping that she'd be able to make the transition. At least two human companions remained with her 24/7 for the next year. When the time finally came to introduce her to the other whales, they refused to accept her. The scene was painful to watch, but necessary if Kayavak was to live as a normal beluga. One morning, the trainers arrived to find Kayavak swimming together with the pod. Now five years old, she still ranks lowest in the hierarchy, but she's tough and feisty and gets along fine.

Museum of Science and Industry★★★

57th St., at S. Lake Shore Dr. 773-684-1414. www.msichicago.org. Open year-round Memorial Day– Labor Day Mon–Sat 9:30am– 5:30pm, Sun 11am–5:30pm. Rest of the year Mon–Sat 9:30am–4pm, Sun 11am–4pm. Closed Dec 25. $13 adults, $9 children (ages 3–11). Free admission days vary by season. Additional charge for Omnimax Theater & special exhibits. By bus, take the #6 Jackson Park Express bus south to 56th St. and walk one block south. In summer, the #10 MSI bus runs right to the museum. Or take Metra train to 57th St. Station and walk east two blocks.

There's a lot here for kids—and adults—to love, and we mean a lot. Here are some of the most popular kid stops. *For more on the MSI, see p48.*

Musts at the MSI

Coal Mine★★ – *Main floor.* A favorite here since 1933, this 20-minute guided tour plunges you from the top of the "headframe" to the "depths" (only a floor down) of a replica coal mine by elevator.

Imaging: Tools of Science★★ – *Main floor.* Computers invite you to manipulate images of your face, create art, and solve crimes.

Toymaker 3000★★ – The best part about this exhibit, intended to teach kids how to create and run a business, is watching a 2,000-square-foot robotic assembly line manufacture 300 tops an hour.

Fairy Castle★ – Furnished with over 1,000 miniatures, the jewel-encrusted Fairy Castle even has running water and electricity. The castle is chock-full of references to familiar fairy tales. Can you find the Bluebird of Happiness?

The Giant Heart★ – Walk through a 13-foot-tall heart (which replaced the 1952 original) and learn how

Science Storms exhibit, Museum of Science and Industry

©J.B. Spector/Museum of Science and Industry Chicago

FOR KIDS

Finnegan's Ice Cream Parlor

If you happen to wander down **Yesterday's Main Street** on the main floor behind the Coal Mine, you might want to "set a spell" at **Finnegan's**. Based on a South Side soda fountain popular in 1917, it serves ice-cream concoctions, sandwiches, and Starbucks® coffee. Main Street itself was installed in 1943, a return to the "good old days" of 1910 intended to take people's minds off World War II.

the beat goes on within us. The heart forms the centerpiece for "You! The Experience," an updated exhibit on cardiac and overall health.

U-505 Submarine★ – Presented in a spectacular setting that explains the history and context of World War II in the North Atlantic Ocean, this German U-boat is the museum's prized artifact. Clever multimedia presentations and compelling films and images rarely seen chronicle the story of its capture off the coast of French West Africa in 1944. Your timed ticket admits you inside the sub, designed to house 56 enlisted men and 4 officers.

Transportation Zone★ – You'll find many of the museum's large vehicles on the main floor, including a cutaway of an actual **Boeing 727★**. The newest star of the gallery is **The Great Train Story★**, where model trains chug around a 3,500-square-foot layout that simulates the busy rail commerce between Chicago and Seattle. Be sure to stop at **All Aboard the Silver Streak★** on the ground floor as you leave for a tour of the **Pioneer Zephyr**, the sleek passenger train that took the West by storm from 1934 to 1960.

Chick Hatchery – Young and old alike are fascinated by watching baby chicks peck their way out of their eggs. Part of the exhibit, Genetics–Decoding Life, the Chick Hatchery is located on the main floor, next to the Transportation Zone.

Idea Factory – *Ground floor; entry by free timed tickets, available at the exhibit entrance.* Very young kids will enjoy this 8,000-square-foot area, loaded with toys and tools for a good time, including a fabulous moat that encircles the space. Next door, 22,000 hand-carved miniature mechanical figures make their way around the **Circus** exhibit.

Henry Crown Space Center – Home of the **Omnimax Theater** *(purchase advance tickets online or by calling the museum)*, this wing also houses the **Apollo 8 command module★**, the first spacecraft ever to circle the moon (1968).

Museum of Science and Industry south façade

© Joe Ziolkowski/Museum of Science and Industry

Chicago Children's Museum

© Chicago Children's Museum

Navy Pier★★ for Kids

600 E. Grand Ave. at Lake Michigan. See p87. For information about free trolleys to Navy Pier, see p15.

If you can keep them out of the candy and ice-cream shops, Navy Pier has rides and amusements that will entertain kids for hours. It won't be cheap, though—each attraction charges its own admission fee. The **Ferris wheel**, a pier landmark, soars up 150 feet, and can sway in the wind on the city's signature windy days. For more excitement, the **Wave Swinger** slings riders through the air. For young kids, there's the old-fashioned **carousel** with its 36 colorful animals.

For some really cheesy fun, try Amazing Chicago's Funhouse Maze or the Time Escape 3D Ride, both of which use special effects to transport you through Chicago as you'll never see it again. The Pier also features a mini-golf course and a Build-A-Bear Workshop, for making stuffed animals. The **Chicago Shakespeare Theater** *(312-595-5600; www.chicagos hakes.com; see p123)* often mounts children's productions.

Chicago Children's Museum★

312-527-1000. www.chichildrens museum.org. Daily 10am–5pm, Thu 10am–8pm. Closed Thanksgiving Day & Dec 25. $12. Free admission Thu after 5pm and first Sunday of the month (ages 15 and under).
The Children's Museum greets visitors as they enter Navy Pier on foot. There's lots to do here for the under-11-year-old set. Three floors of hands-on exhibits invite youngsters to build bridges and forts, invent a flying machine, dig up dinosaur bones, meet giant insects, explore a replica schooner, and even appear on TV. Programs, performances, and workshops (along with happy kids) make this museum a lively place.

Brookfield Zoo★★

8400 W. 31st St., Brookfield. 14mi west of Chicago. 708-688-8000. www.czs.org. Open Memorial Day–Labor Day daily 9:30am–6pm. Rest of the year Mon–Fri 10am–5pm. $13.50 adults, $9.50 children ages 3–11. All-in-one tickets include major attractions at the zoo: $26.50 adults, $20.50 children ages 3–11. Inquire about free days.

FOR KIDS

Hudson polar bear, Brookfield Zoo

©Steve Pine/Chicago Zoological Society/Brookfield Zoo

If you have a day to spend, it's worth the jaunt to this suburban zoo. Its 216 acres fan out around a central fountain, and 15 miles of footpaths wind through the lovely grounds. Shady stretches of lawn invite picnicking. With over 2,800 resident beasts, you'll find all your favorites here, from aardvarks to zebras. Here are several exhibits you and the kids shouldn't miss.

Brookfield Breakdown

Seven Seas★★ – Make a beeline in the morning for the Dolphinarium to see a **Dolphin Presentation**★ *(several 20min performances daily; $2.50 adults, $2 children)*. Later shows tend to get crowded.

Tropic World★★ – Inhabited by primates, this area offers a dramatic treetop perspective of life in the rainforests of Asia, Africa, and South America.

The Fragile Kingdom★ – Clouded leopards, comical meerkats, and naked mole rats occupy habitats that re-create an African desert and an Asian rain forest.

Habitat Africa!★ – Wander from the open savanna to the dense forest, admiring giraffes, okapis, crocodiles, and pythons en route.

Regenstein Wolf Woods – Brookfield's newest habitat, located in the southwestern corner of the zoo, is home to a pack of endangered Mexican gray wolves.

Theater for Kids

These Chicago theaters love kids and kids love them back. Here's a quick overview of a few favorites.

Chicago Kids Company – 773-205-9600. www.chicagokidscompany.com. The company puts on fun plays for kids at various venues.

Emerald City Theatre Company – 773-529-2690. www.emeraldcitytheatre.com. Emerald City offers Cinderella, Wizard of Oz, and the like, usually performed at the Apollo Theater.

Lifeline Theatre – 6912 N. Glenwood Ave. 773-761-4477. www.lifelinetheatre.com. This small neighborhood theater often brings classic kids' books to life.

Vittum Theater – 1012 N. Noble St. 773-342-4141. www.vittumtheater.org. Serious and comic theater performances here are tailored to young audiences.

MUST DO

The pack is most active at the beginning and the end of the day. **The Living Coast** – The shores of Chile and Peru teem with life, with free-flying birds, sliding penguins, and swimming sharks in this popular exhibit.

Lincoln Park Zoo★★

2001 N. Clark St. 312-742-2000. www.lpzoo.org. Open Apr–Oct: grounds open daily 9am–6pm; buildings and farm until 5pm. Nov–Mar: grounds until 5pm, buildings and farm until 4:30pm. Memorial Day–Labor Day weekends and holidays grounds close 7pm, buildings close 6:30pm. Free.

In addition to its penguin and bird houses, bear and cat habitats, and sea lion pool, this accessible zoo's approach is toward replicating natural environments and encouraging natural behavior. From snakes to polar bears, this zoo has it all, and the **Pritzker Family Children's Zoo** is designed to make children feel at home with creatures ranging from snakes to wolves.

Touring Tip

To get to the zoo by car from downtown, drive west on I-290 to the First Avenue exit, then continue south on 1st Avenue to 31st Street and follow signs to the main North Gate parking lot *($8)*. By train, take the Burlington Northern Metra train line from Union Station in the Loop. Get off at the zoo stop at Hollywood Station and walk north two blocks *(fares & schedules: 312-836-7000; www.metrarail.com)*. A good way to see the sprawling zoo is via the 45-minute **Motor Safari Tour** *($3 adults, $2 children)*.

Lincoln Park Lineup

Regenstein Center for African Apes★★ – Gorillas and chimps cavort in their 29,000-square-foot indoor-outdoor home. Watch them play on 5,000 feet of vines, fish for treats in "termite" mounds and scramble around the mud banks. Beware: they're watching you, too. They love to shoot bursts of air at visitors with a giant air gun! You will find the Lester E. Fisher Center at this building, where

Chimpanzee, Lincoln Park Zoo

© Lincoln Park Zoo / Greg Neise

FOR KIDS

all ages can come and learn interactively about wildlife conservation and related initiatives. **Regenstein African Journey★★** – There's a habitat around every corner here, each one part of an African ecosystem—we dare you to step into a dark enclave filled with 10,000 Madagascar hissing cockroaches! Outdoors you can wander through the African savanna with the big guys— giraffes, elephants, ostriches. Kids aged 3–12 can hop on the **LPZoo Children's Train Ride** *($2.50; Mar–Oct 10am–4:40pm)*. On the beautiful **carousel** installed atop the education center, kids can ride their favorite endangered animals *($2.75; open Mar–Oct 10am–4:40pm)*.

Farm-in-the-Zoo Presented by John Deere★ – Here kids can climb aboard a tractor, meet the animals, and feed and milk the cows *(check posters for schedules)*.

🛍 American Girl Place

835 N. Michigan Ave. 877-247-5223. www.american girl.com. Open year-round Mon– Thu 10am–7pm, Fri 10am–9pm, Sat 9am–9pm, Sun 9am–7pm. Closed Thanksgiving Day & Dec 25.

Little girls and their dolls flock to this full-service fantasyland. After you shop the complete line of American Girl dolls and products (including dress-alike clothing for doll and child), the exhibits, cooking classes, theater programs, and reading groups can keep you busy for the rest of the day *(many events require reservations)*. The café *(reservations recommended)* serves brunch, lunch, tea, and dinner; special

Touring Tip

You can park for $12 along Cannon Drive to the east of the grounds *(enter from Fullerton Ave.)*. Pick up maps, audio tours, and strollers in the **Gateway Pavilion** to the north of the main entrance off Cannon Drive. You might also find free parking in Lincoln Park along Stockton Drive to the zoo's west. CTA bus routes 151 and 156 both serve the zoo. If you want to ride around the zoo, hop aboard the **LPZoo Express** *($2.50)*. Park Place Café offers good eats year-round in a food-court setting; or check out Big Cats, Landmark, or Elephant cafés for quick bites in the warmer months. Step outside zoo boundaries to the south for a meal at **Café Brauer** *(see p66)*.

packages are available for birthday parties and even more exclusive events.

Dolls can even have their hair done in the Doll Hair Salon, and girls can have their photo on the cover of an American Girl magazine in the Photo Studio.

For little girls who love their dolls, a trip to AGP is perfect.

🛍 ComedySportz4Kidz

929 W. Belmont Ave. 773-549-8080. www.comedysportzchicago.com. Sat 11am (50min show). $10 adults, $7 children.

Chicago is known for improv comedy. Unfortunately for parents, improv often goes blue, and is typically inappropriate for little ones. ComedySportz has solved that problem, with G-rated shows that actually are funny enough that they don't bore grown-ups.

MUST DO

City of the Big Pizzas

Chicago is one of the country's greatest spots for 'za; aficionados rave about the local deep-dish variety. This savory concoction of tomatoes, cheese, sausage, and vegetables ladled over a thick, doughy crust was developed in the 1940s by restaurateur Ike Sewell, whose restaurants **Pizzeria Uno** *(29 E. Ohio St.; 312-321-1000; www.unos.com)* and **Pizzeria Due** *(619 N. Wabash St.; 312-943-2400; www.unos.com)* still serve the genuine article to crowds of eager eaters. Be prepared to wait; cooking your massive pizza takes around 45 minutes.

♨ Swedish-American Museum and Children's Museum of Immigration

5211 N. Clark St. 773-728-8111. www.samac.org. Open Mon–Thu 1–4pm, Fri 10am–4pm, Sat–Sun 11am–4pm. $4 adults, $3 children, $10 family rate. Free admission second Tue of the month.

Though tiny from the outside, this Andersonville museum provides hours of entertainment for kids (ages 3–12) in its **Brunk Children's Museum of Immigration**. The hands-on facilities give kids a realistic, yet entertaining, look at what it meant to come to the new country, complete with a 20-foot immigrant steamer and a pioneer log cabin. Pre-America takes include a Viking ship and a refugees' raft. Grown-ups can tour the museum's collection of Swedish artifacts and artwork, and shop in the gift shop.

♨ Chicago Children's Theatre

773-227-0180. www.chicago childrenstheatre.org. Varying shows, venues, and ticket prices. Go online or call for more information on current shows.

This itinerant company produces children's theater for kids of

"Jackie and Me," Chicago Children's Theatre

©Michael Brosilow/Chicago Children's Theatre

every age, including babies and toddlers who can enjoy interactive theater experiences from the safety of their parents' laps. Preteen and teen-friendly shows are also a staple. Company productions occur in various venues, from Victory Gardens' Biograph to the Ruth Page Center to Millennium Park and the North Shore Center for the Performing Arts.

Mitchell Museum of the American Indian
See p57.
3001 Central St., Evanston.

SHOPPING

Forget any doubts you may have about Chicago's fashion sense: you can shop this town 'til you drop. Add a dose of Midwestern good sense and practicality, and a touch of innovation on a manageable scale, and you have a city where high-style boutiques rub shoulders with bargain basements, vintage treasure troves, and farmers' markets.

Magnificent Mile★★★

Beverly Hills has Rodeo Drive, New York has Madison Avenue, and Chicago has the Mag Mile. North Michigan Avenue is indisputably *the* shopping promenade in the city. As you stroll the lovely avenue from the river to **Oak Street★** *(see opposite page)*, you'll notice that Mag Mile has fallen victim to the homogenizing effect of contemporary retailing—chain stores like **Crate and Barrel**, **Williams-Sonoma**, **Banana Republic**, and **Gap** now mingle with the exclusive boutiques and historic architectural façades. Even so, time spent shopping here will certainly not disappoint the acquisition-minded. Who could resist tony Dallas retailer **Neiman Marcus** (*737 N. Michigan Ave.; 312-642-5900; www. neimanmarcus.com*)? Then there's **Filene's Basement** (*830*

N. Michigan Ave.; 312-482-8918; www.filenesbasement.com), the country's oldest off-price department store; Swedish fave **H&M** (*840 N. Michigan Ave.; 312-640-0060; www.hm.com*); and **Niketown Chicago** (*669 N. Michigan Ave.; 312-642-6363; www.niketown.nike.com*), which offers clothing for every sport along with seasonal celeb appearances. **Crate and Barrel** may be a chain, but it is Chicago's chain, with local roots. Check out their flagship store (*646 N. Michigan Ave.; 312-787-5900; www.crateandbarrel.com*).

Mag Mile Malls

Vertical malls add scores of stores and restaurants to the possibilities along North Michigan Avenue (malls below are listed from south to north).

North Bridge – *520 N. Michigan Ave. 312-327-2300. www.theshops atnorthbridge.com*. Fifty shops, 20 restaurants, five hotels, and a four-level shopping center (Nordstrom) fill this attractive mall, where the third floor is devoted exclusively to kids. This is the home of the Seattle retailer **Nordstrom**, which made the Chicago scene in 2000.

600 North Michigan Shops – *600 N. Michigan Ave. 312-266-5630*. Eddie Bauer is a highlight here, along with a multiplex movie theater.

Chicago Place – *700 N. Michigan Ave. 312-266-7710. www.chicago-*

Chicago Place

© David Dunai/Apa Publications Ltd.

New Maxwell Street Market

Canal St. at Roosevelt Rd. Park for $3 at Clinton St. & 14th Pl. Open year-round Sun 7am–3pm. 312-922-3100. Chicago's oldest outdoor market dates back to the late 19C when Jewish immigrants ran a bustling open-air bazaar here. Although the market and its vendors and shoppers have changed over the years, the place always remained gritty and urban. Today, urban renewal has taken its toll, and the new, sanitized Maxwell Street Market is but a shadow of its former self. Still, more than 480 vendors peddle their wares—from produce to antiques—and street performers and musicians entertain.

place.com. **Saks Fifth Avenue** anchors these eight levels, which include **Ann Taylor** and **Talbots**. Drop by delightful **Chiaroscuro**, a gallery of colorful, funky eclectica, with items you can't find everywhere else.

Water Tower Place★ – *835 N. Michigan Ave. 312-440-3166. www.shopwatertower.com.* Water Tower Place boasts the largest selection of all, from department-store chain **Macy's** and favorites **Abercrombie & Fitch** and **Hollister Co.** to the local flair of **The Oprah Store** and **Chicago Cubs Clubhouse Shop**.

The 900 Shops – *900 N. Michigan Ave. 312-915-3916. www.shop900.com.* Swankiest of the Mag Mile malls, 900 North Michigan includes a six-story **Bloomingdale's**, plus **Gucci** and **Michael Kors** among its 70 stores. Other favorites at this landmark establishment include Alternatives Shoes (*www.altshoes.com*), a great source for hip shoes, and Mark Shale (*www.markshale.com*), the locally owned option for classic workwear for both men and women.

Magnificent Shopping Streets

Oak Street★ – *West side of Michigan Ave., one block north of Walton Pl.* Hunting for haute couture? Duck down Oak Street, where you'll flush out a wonderful array of designer boutiques, jewelry stores, and intimate shops. Bag the hippest fashions at **VINCE** *(no. 106; 312-280-6890; www. vince.com)* and **Prada** *(no. 30; 312-951-1113, www.prada.com)*, or shoot for quintessentially elegant accessories at **Hermès of Paris** *(no. 110; 312-787-8175; www.hermes. com)* or **Yves St. Laurent Rive Gauche** *(no. 51; 312-751-8895; www.ysl.com)*. Anchoring all this glamor is **Barneys New York** *(no. 25; 312-587-1700; www.barneys. com)*. Buyers beware: these trendy shops are not for the faint of budget. One exception is the fabulous **Bravco** *(no 43; 312-943-*

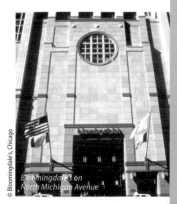

© Bloomingdale's, Chicago

Bloomingdale's on North Michigan Avenue

SHOPPING

4305; www.bravcobeauty.com; pay by cash only). This two-story beauty supply shop has brands of beauty products at cheaper prices, but without that icky outlet feel. Salon and spa treatments are available at Charles Ifergan, Marianne Strokirk, Marilyn Miglin, Exhale, and The Spa on Oak.

State Street★ – *Between Randolph & Adams Sts.* Chicago's first retail corridor, State Street's fortunes in the Loop have soared and dipped over the years. For years that Great Street housed two of Chicago's most famous homegrown retailers. That's no longer the case. The former flagship Marshall Field's is now **Macy's★** *(111 N. State St.; see p26),* and the former home to Carson, Pirie, Scott & Company Store *(1 S. State St.; see p23)* is now the restored Sullivan Center, soon to host a new Target. The Nordstrom Rack, Sears, and Urban Outfitters are among the other retail outlets on State Street.

Armitage Avenue – *Between Halsted St. & Racine Ave.; lincolnparkshopping.com.* Stroll this historic district, with its lovely residences, boutiques, and eateries. Stop by **Tabula Tua** *(1015 W. Armitage Ave.; 773-525-3500;*

www.tabulatua.com) for luscious table settings and other home accessories; Chicago womenswear by **Lori's Designer Shoes** *(824 W. Armitage Ave.; 773-281-5655; www.lorisshoes.com)* for selection and price. Locals also flock to **Fox's Designer Off-Price** *(2150 N. Halsted St.; 773-281-0700; www. foxs.com),* which offers exactly what its name says. **Mint Julep** *(1013 W. Armitage Ave.; 773-296-2997)* is a funky local clothing boutique. There is no question that you'll be the only person on your block with your handbag if you buy it at **1154 Lill** *(904 W. Armitage Ave.; 773-477-5455; www.1154lill. com),* because you'll design your own. 1154 has purse patterns and fabrics and ships you your one-of-a-kind creation once it is sewn. In recent years this strip has evolved from local boutiques to nationally known outposts. You'll find designers like **Cynthia Rowley** *(808 W. Armitage Ave.; 773-528-6160; www.cynthiarowley.com)* and **Barneys New York COOP** *(2209 N. Halsted St.; 773-248-0426; www.barneys.com).*

Southport Avenue – *Between Belmont Ave. & Irving Park Rd.* When local boutiques got priced off of Lincoln Park's Armitage Avenue *(see left)* they fled to Lakeview's Southport Avenue, which has become one of the city's best shopping areas. For close to a decade **Krista K** *(3458 N. Southport Ave., 773-248-1967, kristak.com)* has been the strip's favorite stop for fashionable women's clothes and, now, maternity clothes, too. **Red Head Boutique** *(3450 N. Southport Ave.; 773-325-9898)* stocks hot local designers and

Macy's

Courtesy of Macy's

Swedish-American Museum

The Swedish-American Museum

room for furnishings in your suitcase, or you are willing to have things shipped, you cannot miss **Scout** *(5221 N. Clark St.; 773 -275-5700; www.scoutchicago.com)* for a well-edited antique décor. **Haus** *(5405 N. Clark St.; 773-769-4000: www.hauschicago.com)* has contemporary art and décor items that are made in small quantities. Reward all your hard retail work with a rare Belgian beer or microbrew at **Hopleaf** *(5148 N. Clark St.; 773-334-9851; hopleaf.com)*, with 50 brews on tap, hundreds by the bottle and a full dinner menu.

Women and Children First *(5233 N. Clark St; 773-769 9299; www.womenandchildrenfirst.com)* is not just a bookstore, rather it is a neighborhood icon with plenty of authors' readings, as well as a remarkable selection of books for women and kids.

Damen and Milwaukee Avenues – *Between Webster & Division Aves.* Much of the trendy retail action of artsy **Bucktown/ Wicker Park** happens along Bucktown's Damen and Milwaukee Avenues. Try **p.45** *(1643 N. Damen Ave.; 773-862-4523; www.p45.com)* for edgy women's fashion from

there's something for everyone at funky **Uncle Fun** *(1338 W. Belmont Ave.; 773-477-8223; www.unclefunchicago.com)*, right around the corner on Belmont Avenue.

Clark Street – *Between Foster & Bryn Mawr Aves.* Swedish in its origins, **Andersonville** *(www. andersonville.org)* has grown popular and eclectic in its shopping opportunities; you'll find antiques, hip and chic home accessories and gifts here. For a Scandinavian fix, drop by the gift shop at the **Swedish-American Museum** *(5211 N. Clark St.; 773-728-8111; www.samac.org; see p101)*, loaded with Kosta Boda crystal and other Swedish specialties. If you have

Farmers' Markets

Chicago prides itself on its neighborhood farmers' markets, which bring the bounty of the surrounding countryside into the city from May through October *(check at www.egov.cityofchicago.org for times and locations)*. Foodies should check out **Chicago's Green City Market** *(1750 N. Clark St., at Stockton Dr., in Lincoln Park; open mid-May–Oct Wed and Sat 7am–1pm; 773-435-0280; www.chicagogreencitymarket.org)*. This nonprofit market was created to support the sustainable and organic food movements in Chicago and to provide fresh local produce to an increasing number of restaurateurs. Operating since 1999, the Green Market is open to the public and features at least 50 vendors of heirloom fruits and vegetables along with cooking demonstrations by prominent local chefs.

SHOPPING

Mart Smart

Chicago's wholesale furniture and design behemoth, the **Merchandise Mart** *(222 Merchandise Mart Plaza, River North; open Mon–Fri 9am–6pm; 312-527-4141; www.merchandisemart.com)* is second in size only to the Pentagon in Washington, DC. Most of the Mart is open only to card-carrying professionals, but the new **LuxeHome** boutiques welcome the public as well. Located on the first floor of the Mart and accessible by all entrances, LuxeHome includes 70,000 square feet and 25 kitchen and bath showrooms, featuring everything from fixtures to stonework. Check out the latest from Poggenpohl, Waterworks, de Giulio, and others. Not in the market for a new Jacuzzi? Take a 90-minute tour of the wholesale merchandisers *(Mon & Fri 1pm; $12)*.

Chicago's best young designers. Local designers shine bright at **Eskell** *(1509 N. Milwaukee Ave.; 773-486-0837; eskell.com)*. **Robin Richman** *(2108 N. Damen Ave.; 773-278-6150)* is a local dress designer with an eponymous boutique and a terrific eye. **Viva La Femme** *(2048 N. Damen Ave.; 773-772-7429; www.vivela femme.com)* is a rare bird: a store designed for curvy and plus-size women that is hip and fashionable and fun. Walls and walls of color-coordinated ribbon deck the halls at **Soutache** *(2125 N. Damen Ave.; 773-292-9110; soutacheribbons. com)*. It is a paradise for crafty types. Shop for 18C and 19C Chinese furniture at **Pagoda Red** *(1714 N. Damen Ave.; 773-235-1188; www.pagodared.com)*. **Division Street** – Boutiques and funky shops line the main thoroughfare of nearby **Ukrainian Village**. Edgy and trendy are bywords at boutiques like **Bonnie & Clyde's** *(1751 W. Division St.; 773-235-2860)*, **Le Dress** *(1741 W. Division St., 773-697-9899)*, **Strut** *(1744 W. Division St., 773-227-2728)*, and **Noir** *(1726 W. Division St., 773-572-6084)*, which only offers black clothing. **Nina** *(1655 W Division St.; 773-486-*

8996; www.ninachicago.com) has a minimalist esthetic, setting it apart from almost any other yarn and knitting store you've entered. **The Ruby Room** *(1743-45 W. Division St.; 773-235-2323; www.rubyroom.com; see p111)* is a spa with an impressive retail section. Come here for alternative skin care and make-up, as well as books, crystals, and even quirky items like dog collars that change color based on your pup's mood. **Devon Avenue** – *Between Western & California Aves*. The "Midwest capital of gold dealers" hosts 20 jewelers selling mostly 22- and 24-karat gold jewelry. The formerly Jewish area has become the heart of Chicago's Indian community, featuring restaurants and colorful sari shops, with the Bollywood-style designer shop **Raaz** *(2317 W. Devon Ave., 773-764-9501)* leading the pack. Get the movies themselves at **India Book House/ Atlantic Video** *(2551 W. Devon Ave., 773-338-3600)* or find bangles to match every outfit at **Sahiba Boutique** *(2614 W. Devon Ave., 773-4645-1900)*. Parking is tough in this area at night, but the energy and the great people-watching opportunities make up for any frustration. Shops tend to be open late here.

Wentworth Avenue – *South of Cermak Rd., in Chinatown.* A wonderful place to while away the afternoon, Chicago's **China-town** offers shops, groceries, bakeries, and restaurants aplenty. Stores carry the usual interesting mix of American, Chinese, and Japanese goods, including silk bathrobes, jackets and traditional dresses, ceramics, tea, and toys. **Woks 'n Things** *(2234 S. Wentworth Ave.; 312-842-0701)* stocks an amazing array of cookware. Be sure to roam the blocks west of Wentworth for more shops.

Lincoln Avenue – *Between Lawrence Ave. & Montrose Ave.* **Lincoln Square** *(www.lincoln square.org; see p33)* was once the enclave for German immigrants to Chicago. There are still vestiges of that population here, but its shopping reaches out to a much more diverse crowd. Stop at **Quake Collectibles** *(4628 N. Lincoln Ave.; 773-878-4288)* for nostalgic items from your youth, including action figures and lunch boxes. **The Dressing Room** *(4635 N. Lincoln Ave.; 773-728-0088; www. thedressingroomchicago.com)* has quickly become a must-shop for local women. **Traipse** *(4341 N. Lincoln Ave.; 773-935-5511; www.traipseshoes.com)* stocks high-end, yet comfortable and wearable imported shoes. Sweet-smelling soaps and body washes are just part of the appeal at neighborhood icon **Merz Apothecary** *(4716 N. Lincoln Ave.; 773-989-0900; www.smallflower.com)*. On-staff pharmacists help you make sense of the alternative health and beauty projects stocked here. Take a load off your feet at the combination bookstore and wine bar **Book Cellar** *(4736 N. Lincoln Ave.; 773-293-2665; www.bookcellarinc.com)*.

River North Galleries

The **River North Gallery District** *(bounded on the east and west by N. Wells & N. Orleans Sts., and on the south and north by W. Huron St. & W. Chicago Ave.)* vies with Manhattan's Soho for claiming the largest concentration of art galleries. Clustered along and around Superior Street, galleries, antique shops, and home-furnishings stores—many of which occupy 19C warehouses—provide the perfect setting to find that piece of art that you just can't live without.On certain Friday evenings each month, galleries open their new shows *(for schedules check*

Book Cellar, Chicago

online at www.chicagogallerynews. com or pick up a free copy of *Chicago Gallery News*). If you're adding to your contemporary art collection, here's a few galleries to get you started: **Andrew Bae Gallery** – *300 W. Superior St. 312-335-8601. www.andrewbaegallery.com*. Andrew Bae specializes in contemporary and young Asian artists. **Carl Hammer Gallery** – *740 N.Wells St. 312-266-8512. www.hammergallery.com*. "Outsider" and self-taught artists are featured here. **Catherine Edelman** – *300 W. Superior St. 312-266-2350. www.edelmangallery. com*. This is one of the Midwest's leading galleries devoted exclusively to photography. **ArchiTech** – *730 N. Franklin St. 312-475-1290. www.architech gallery.com*. Chicago's only gallery of architectural art, drawings, and prints. **Perimeter Gallery** – *210 W. Superior St. 312-266-9473. www.perimetergallery.com*. Perimeter offers contemporary painting, sculpture, works on paper, and master crafts. **Zolla/Lieberman Gallery** – *325 W. Huron St. 312-944-1990. www.zollaliebermangallery.com*. The first gallery to come to River North, in 1975, showcases contemporary works by emerging and established artists.

West Loop Galleries

Douglas Dawson's move of his eponymous **Douglas Dawson Gallery** *(400 N. Morgan St.; 312-226-7975; www.douglas dawson.com)* from River North to the West Loop is one of the things that proved to people that the West Loop was for serious galleries and collectors. Today is it an enclave for avant-garde galleries as well as those who simply decided to stop paying River North prices. As in River North, there are open gallery strolls on the first Thursday of the spring and summer months at 5–7pm. Stop at Douglas Dawson for some of the best ethnographic art in the country. Fans of ceramics will enjoy **Dubhe Carreno Gallery** *(118 N. Peoria, 2nd floor.; 773-931-6584; www.dubhecarreno gallery.com)*, while Ground Zero for pop art is **Mars Gallery** *(1139 W. Fulton Mkt.; 312-226-7808; www.marsgallery.com)*. Down the block the **Linda Warren Gallery** *(130 N. Jefferson St.; 312-575-9600; www.lindawarrengallery.com)* exhibits emerging artists who aren't often shown in Chicago. **Primitive** *(1052 W. Fulton Mkt.; 312-432-0100; www.beprimitive. com)* sells furniture, artifacts, art, textiles, jewelry, and fashion from all over the world. Check your calendar before you visit the neighborhood: If the dates and times line up, both the **Chicago Antique Market** *(1340 W. Washington St.; www.chicago antiquemarket.com)* and **Leslie Hindman Auctioneers** *(1338 W. Lake St.; 312-280-1212; www.leslie hindman.com)* are good places to find one-of-a-kind treasures, often for bargain prices.

South Loop

For too long the South Loop was just somewhere south of all the action, but nowhere you'd want to go. Now, it is a vibrant neighborhood, a destination in its own right. One of the strengths is the bookstore mecca that is Printers Row. Try **Sandmeyer's Book Store** *(714 S. Dearborn St.;*

312-922-2104) and **Printers Row Fine and Rare** *(715 S. Dearborn St.; 312-583-1800)*, the city's oldest surviving antiquarian and rare bookshop. Knitters will love **Loopy Yarns** *(47 W. Polk St., 312-583-9276)*. Other growth has come in the University Village end of the neighborhood, home to **Southgate Market** *(1101 S. Canal St.)*, a sustainable shopping center. **Flaunt Boutique** *(75 E. 16th St.; 312-360-1000)* is the neighborhood favorite for women's clothing, along with high-end funky chic **Gourmet Clothing** *(1252 S. Halsted St.; 312-997-2411)*. **Lush Wine & Spirits** *(1306 S. Halsted St.; 312-738-1900)* is a great alternative to fussy wine shops.

Hyde Park

Hyde Park's academic roots, thanks to the University of Chicago, shine through when it comes to shopping. While there is plenty of diversity, the strength of the neighborhood shopping is its bookstores, both new and used. Your first stop must be **Seminary Co-op Bookstore** *(5757 S. University Ave.; 773-752-4381)*, chock-full of any book you could want and many more that you've never heard of. Run by the same folks who own Seminary, **57th Street Books** *(1301 E. 57th St.; 773-684-1300)* has more general interest and children's books. **Powell's Books** *(1501 E. 57th St.; 773-955-7780)* is for those who prefer used books, and the treasure-hunting process of finding them. **Artisans 21** *(1373 E. 53rd St., 773-288-7450)* is one of the oldest cooperative art galleries. A good selection of new and used vinyl and CDs can

be found at **Hyde Park Records** *(1377 E. 53rd St., 773-288-6588)*.

Bargains at Outlet Mall Shopping

If you have access to a car and really want a bargain, consider driving to one of several outlet malls in the greater Chicago area. All of them have stores from major national designers at discount prices, some with more in-season goods than others.

Clothes

For the best selection of designer clothes, try **Chicago Premium Outlets Mall** *(1650 Premium Outlets Blvd., Aurora; 630-585-2200)*. **Gurnee Mills Outlet Mall** *(6170 W. Grand Ave., Gurnee; 847-263-7500)* has something for everyone, including the perk of being across the street from an amusement park. There are play areas, movie theaters, and other entertainment, in addition to shopping. **Prime Outlets Huntley Mall** *(11800 Factory Shops Blvd., Huntley; 847-669-9100)* – Though smaller than Chicago Premium, this place also has designer clothing and home décor shops.

Local stores with outlets

Some local stores also have their own outlets in the city, including furniture heavyweight **Crate & Barrel** *(1864 N. Clybourn Ave.; 312-787-4775)* and **Madison and Friends Outlet** *(1963 N. Halsted St.; 312-943-0436)*, which stocks denim for kids and tweens. Dish towels and table lines can be scooped up at the Tag brand outlet, **1730 Outlet Company** *(1730 W. Wrightwood Ave.; 773-871-4331; www.1730outlet.com)*.

SHOPPING

SPAS

Need a vacation from your vacation? Chicago has just the thing. Slip away for a couple of hours—or make a day of it—and indulge yourself at one of the city's many pampering palaces.

⚜ Asha

55 E. Ontario St., Magnificent Mile. 312-664-0200. www.ashasalonspa.com.

Asha has become the Aveda spa heavyweight in Chicago, with six locations in the city and suburbs, including on the Gold Coast and in Bucktown. A favorite indulgence is the location at the **James Chicago** *(see p141)*, where the service is even more attentive than usual. Despite the chain's size, you are sure to get personalized care here. Weary travelers who struggle with keeping healthy on airplanes should try the sinus-friendly Neti Massage.

Charles Ifergan

106 E. Oak St., Magnificent Mile. 312-642-4484. www.charles ifergan.com.

This establishment was among the first businesses on Oak Street, and today its friendly staff offers expert salon and spa services. Whether you get the works in a Day of Beauty or just go for a two-hour Executive Treatment, you'll emerge feeling like a whole new person.

Elizabeth Arden Red Door Salon and Spa

919 N. Michigan Ave. (enter on Walton St.), Magnificent Mile. 312-988-9191. www.reddoorspas.com.

The grand dame of all spas, and the classic choice of Chicago's most pampered, Elizabeth Arden's Red Door delivers skin care, massage, hydrotherapy, and more with panache. Try an Elemental Balancing massage, in which aromatherapy oils are custom blended for you.

Exhale

945 N. State St., Gold Coast. 312-753-6500. www.exhalespa.com.

This light-filled spa near Oak Street is all luxury. Whether you are looking for beauty treatments, spa treatments, or some serious yoga instruction, Exhale is the place to relax and take a deep breath. **Note:** *Exhale is popular with locals, so call as far ahead as possible to make appointments.*

Nurture in Nature

Ensconced in beautiful Illinois farm country, **Heartland Spa** is a healthy jaunt from Chicago, but worth the trip if you'd like to concentrate a few days on improving your fitness through exercise, diet, and stress relief *(90 miles south of Chicago, off I-57 South; 1237 E. 1600 North Rd., Gilman, IL; 815-683-2182 or 800-545-4853; www.heartlandspa.com)*. You can take aerobic and strength classes, tai chi and yoga, and enjoy a full range of body treatments.

MUST DO

Massage at Exhale

Exhale Spa, Chicago

🛁 Kiva Spa & Salon

196 E. Pearson St.,
Magnificent Mile. 312-840-8120.
www.premierspacollection.com.

Spa aficionados may recognize
Kiva's parent company, the Premier
Collection of Spas, with locations
coast to coast. In Chicago, the
southwestern surroundings
are relaxing and welcoming. In
addition to standard spa services,
Kiva offers reflexology, cocoon
therapies (choose from Ayurvedic,
marine, mother earth, and more),
and treatments for men.

Mario Tricoci

900 N. Michigan Ave.,
Magnificent Mile. 800-874-2624.
www.tricoci.com.

Big, bold cousin of the **Red Door**
(both are owned by Elizabeth
Arden), Tricoci has locations all over
the Chicago area, particularly in the
suburbs. This huge facility offers
everything from Spa-on-the-Go to
the MT Signature Day of Beauty,
among other packages.
Or choose polishes, wraps,
massages, hair, make-up, and
nail services à la carte.

Paradise Sauna

2910 W. Montrose Ave.,
Lincoln Square. 773-588-3304.

A traditional Korean spa, Paradise
is not fancy by any stretch of the
imagination. But the hot and cold
dipping pools and well-trained
massage therapists make this a
great place for some hard-core
R&R for both men and women
(in segregated areas).
Note: You must pay the fee to
use the pools if you come for a
treatment (massage and body
scrubs), so you should plan on
using them.

Peninsula Spa

108 E Superior St.,
Magnificent Mile. 312-573-6860.
www.peninsula.com.

Those who are serious about
being pampered know to turn to
one of the most luxurious hotels
in the city for one of its most
luxurious spa experiences. This is
not for the budget-minded.
Note: Everything at the Peninsula
is pricy, although worth it if you
like to indulge. Favorites include
couples massages in your hotel
room as well as treatments near
the mosiac-adorned pool. Keep
your eyes open: You may see
some celebrities here.

The Ruby Room

1743-45 W. Division St.,
Ukrainian Village. 773-235-2323.
www.rubyroom.com.

This is a high-end spa with a
holistic attitude. If you are curious
about alternative therapies, but
have been wary, this is a great place
for a first-time treatment. Choose

SPAS

Thousand Waves Spa for Women

©Jennie Gunnerson/Thousand Waves Spa for Women

For women only, this serene, Japanese-style spa offers massages provided by women trained in a variety of techniques. Herbal wraps come in flavors from white pine bark to rosebud. All treatments begin in the three baths—dry sauna, eucalyptus steam, and Jacuzzi sauna. If you only want to access the baths, no appointment is needed.

from massage and skin treatments or more esoteric energy healing. Your interest in and comfort level with the New Age material guides the staff.

Spa Space

161 N. Canal St., Near West Side. 312-466-9585. www.spaspace.com.

This spa caters to busy professionals and offers a full line for men (Space Men, that is), including sports pedicures and back facials. With advance warning, meals or snacks can be ordered from restaurant Nine's spa menu, and the spa has its own juice bar.

Thousand Waves Spa for Women

1212 W. Belmont Ave., Lakeview. 773-549-0700. www.thousandwavesspa.com.

Urban Oasis

©Micheal Lapin/Urban Oasis

Tiffani Kim Institute

310 W. Superior St., River North. 312-260-9000. Also in Park Hyatt Hotel, 800 N. Michigan Ave., Magnificent Mile; 312-335-1234. www.tiffanikiminstitute.com.

A smorgasbord of therapies, body treatments, and relaxation awaits you at one of Tiffani Kim's two locations (the Park Hyatt spa includes a hair salon). Couples, best friends, and moms and daughters can book specialty services for two, such as facials and massages. And, the Institute even has a line of services for teens, both boys and girls. If you're in the market for a bridal gown, check out Tiffani Kim's stunning line of original designs.

Urban Oasis

939 W. North Ave. (garden level), Old Town; 312-640-0001. Also at 12 W. Maple St. (3rd floor), Gold Coast; 312-587-3500. www.urbanoasis.biz.

Massages are the order of the day here; from reiki and shiatsu, to hot-stone and deep-tissue, you'll find whatever your tired body needs. Try the salt glow, an exhilarating exfoliation treatment, followed by a 30-minute massage.

MUST DO

NIGHTLIFE

The blues rule in Chicago, and jazz is vice-president. There are plenty of venues to hear both, as well as other types of music—reggae, rock, house, and hip-hop. Dance, drink, lounge to your heart's content, upscale or down. Oh, and there's a little comedy club here called The Second City, along with others in both stand-up and ensemble style.

Blues Clubs

Blue Chicago
536 N. Clark St.; 312-661-0100. Nightly 8pm–1:30am, Saturdays until 2:30am. Cover charge $8 Sun–Thu, $10 Fri–Sat. www.bluechicago.com.
This River North club is not your typical funky blues club, but they offer excellent blues in the Chicago tradition at a convenient location.

B.L.U.E.S.
2519 N. Halsted St., Lincoln Park. 773-528-1012. Sun–Fri 8pm–2am, Sat 8pm–3am. www.chicagoblues bar.com.
You feel as though you can reach out and touch the performers in this tiny, atmospheric club. Quality musicians from across the city and a down-and-dirty atmosphere make this one of the most popular blues bars in town. On Sundays, one cover charge gets you into both B.L.U.E.S. and Kingston Mines across the street.

Kingston Mines
2548 N. Halsted St., Lincoln Park. 773-477-4646. www.kingstonmines.com.
Frequented by top-notch musicians and regular folk, this ramshackle blues club features live music until 4am (5am on Saturday). Every night, two top local bands take turns playing on the club's two stages. The place fills up quickly, and at 2am fans pour in from B.L.U.E.S. across the street, so arrive early to get a good seat.

Buddy Guy's Legends
700 S. Wabash Ave., South Loop. Mon–Fri 11am–2am, Sat 5pm–3am, Sun 6pm–2am. 312-427-1190.

Blue Chicago

© Mark Montgomery/City of Chicago

Singin' the Blues

Born in the dusty cotton fields of the Mississippi River delta, the musical genre called the Blues evolved from African slave chants, work songs, and spirituals into a uniquely American musical form. From the hollows, fields, and churches of the rural South, migrants brought their music north to Chicago in the 1910s. As artists such as "Big Bill" Broonzy and "Papa" Charlie Jackson began to play together, a hybrid guitar-driven style based on urban themes emerged. In the 1940s musicians experimented with amplification, and by 1950 Chicago surfaced as the capital of the hard-driving electric blues, with Muddy Waters (McKinley Morganfield) as its king. Today, Chicago greats like B.B. King, Otis Rush, Buddy Guy, and others push the blues into the 21C.

Blues headliners take the stage here around 10:30pm, but earlier audiences on Friday and Saturday are treated to free acoustic sets beginning at 6pm.

House of Blues
329 N. Dearborn St., River North. 312-923-2000. www.houseof blues.com.
Blues is big business here, along with classic rock, heavy metal, and other genres. Try the Gospel Brunch with two seatings every Sunday *(9:30am & noon)* for a rockin' good time.

Jazz Clubs

Andy's Jazz Club
11 E. Hubbard St.,
Magnificent Mile. 312-642-6805.
www.andysjazzclub.com.
This one's a classic, and it offers jazz three times a day: at lunch, the cocktail hour, and mid-evening. The food's not bad here, either.

Green Mill Jazz Club
4802 N. Broadway Ave.,
Uptown. 773-878-5552.
www.greenmilljazz.com.
Al Capone's crew used to hang

Andy's Jazz Club

Andy's Jazz Club

Green Mill Jazz Club

out in this charming jazz club; the interior looks much as it did back in the 1920s and 30s. Jazz acts perform seven nights a week, and the music plays until 4am (5am on Saturday). On Sunday evenings, thick-skinned poets read their works to the crowds who attend the infamous Uptown Poetry Slam competitions.

Close Up2
416 S. Clark St., The Loop. Live music Wed–Sat; 312-385-1111. www.closeupjazz2.com.
This elegant and convenient club showcases "smooth jazz."

Jazz Showcase
806 S. Plymouth Court, The Loop. 312-360-0234. www.jazzshowcase.com.
"Where Jazz Lives in Chicago"— and how. Since 1947 Joe Segal's been bringing jazz stars to his stage to the delight of Chicagoans. There's even a Sunday matinee where kids get in free *(4pm).*

New Checkerboard Lounge for Blues 'n' Jazz
5201 S. Harper Ct., Hyde Park. 773-684-1472.
This is the new, re-opened location of a long-time Hyde Park (and Chicago) favorite. As its name suggests, you'll hear blues and jazz, and some of the best in the city at that. Names like Prince and Keith Richards played at the old Bronzeville location. That may not be happening in Hyde Park, but the club still attracts talented musicians. Expect a diverse crowd, from young to old, thanks to the proximity to the University of Chicago campus. Sundays are a jazz bargain at $10 (cash only).

Pops for Champagne
601 N. State St., Magnificent Mile. 312-266-7677. www.popsfor champagne.com.
Elegant and sophisticated, but not snooty, Pops makes for special nights out. With more than 100 champagnes and live jazz every night, a fireplace in winter, and a store where you can shop for

NIGHTLIFE

Jimmy's Woodlawn Tap

1172 E. 55th St., Hyde Park.
773-643-5516.

This dimly lit tavern is the off-campus hangout for University of Chicago types. Jimmy's prices are low, the beer selection is good, and the bartenders are friendly, so drop by for a cold one (and live jazz on Sunday nights).

bubbly to take home, Pops sparkles for appetizers or dessert. On the North Side, visit the **Star Bar** *(2934 N. Sheffield Ave., Lakeview. 773-472-7272).*

Music and Dance Clubs

Double Door

1572 N. Milwaukee Ave.,
Wicker Park. 773-489-3160.
www.doubledoor.com.

This is the premier live music venue in the area. The owners book bands that are just breaking onto the national scene, and the small, V-shaped room is a great place to see future stars up-close.

Empty Bottle

1035 N. Western Ave., Wicker Park.
773-276-3600.

The Empty Bottle books an eclectic mix of experimental jazz, hot local rock acts, and bands on the brink of national renown.

Enclave

220 W. Chicago Ave.,
River North. 312-644-0234.
www.enclavechicago.com.

If you want to dance the night away, head to Enclave, a warehouse-turned-dance club with plenty of room on the dance

floor and interesting art on the walls. The signature drinks at the bar aren't bad either.

Excalibur

632 N. Dearborn St., River North.
312-266-1944.

Housed in the old Chicago Historical Society, the spacious Excalibur offers something for everyone: eating, dancing, and 12 separate bars ranging over three floors. Music options run from live to DJ, alternative to rock.

Funky Buddha Lounge

728 W. Grand Ave., River West.
312-666-1695. www.funky
buddha.com.

This crowded, too-cool (and possibly too-loud) dance lounge features DJ or live music—jazz, Latin, hip-hop, and house—along with a retro-Zen eclectic scene.

Liar's Club

1665 W. Fullerton Ave., Lakeview.
773-665-1110.

It looks like a dive bar from the outside. In fact, one of the city's best, least pretentious nightclubs rages inside. There is a tiny, yet active, dance floor, moving to sounds spun by a DJ. Music ranges from 70s, 80s, and 90s tunes, while a disco ball hangs above. The upstairs has a pool table and a more low-key vibe. Expect to pay a $5 cover on weekends.

Lumen

839 W. Fulton Mkt., West Loop.
312-733-2222. www.lumen-
chicago.com.

A nightclub that tries to combine the best of both worlds, Lumen offers a see-and-be-seen

atmosphere, but without the VIP sections and long lines.
The interior is sleek and minimalist and the lights, video, and audio are all state-of-the-art. Music tends toward hip-hop and dance music. The dress code prohibits ball caps and flip-flops.

Metro
3730 N. Clark St., Lakeview. 773-549-0203. www.metrochicago.com.
Metro is not new, having taken up space near Wrigley Field since 1983. But, as other clubs come and go, Metro remains hip. With a mission to bring emerging musical artists to town, it still has its finger on the pulse. See bands ranging from little-known Nashville start-ups to bigger names like The White Stripes and the Yeah Yeah Yeahs. Cover charge depends on the band. Downstairs you'll find **Smart Bar**, an always-packed dance club.

Paramount Room
415 N. Milwaukee Ave., River West. 312-829-6300. www.paramount room.com.
Part gastropub, part late-night hang-out, this bar (with better-than-average bar food, including the $10 Kobe burger) transforms as the evening wears on.
There's a DJ on weekends, and occasionally live music, and always a crowd of locals.

The Violet Hour
1520 N. Damen Ave., Wicker Park. 773-252-1500, www.theviolet hour.com.
The inspiration for The Violet Hour was the pre-Prohibition Era, and Chicagoans have been flocking here as if there is nowhere else to get a drink other than their own bathtubs. The creative cocktail menu is impressive, but not speedy, as each drink is made with care. This is one of the few clubs in Chicago where it is hard to find the exterior door, although looking for the crowds should be your first clue: No reservations are taken and no one is let in if every chair is full. The dress code at this speakeasy is relatively basic; no ball caps or cell phones are allowed.

Subterranean
2011 W. North Ave., Wicker Park. 773- 278-6600. www.paramount room.com.
This popular Wicker Park club is actually located above ground. The first floor offers dinner and deejays while the upstairs Cabaret Room hosts live acts of all stripes, tending toward alternative and pop.

Schuba's
3159 N. Southport Ave., Lakeview. 773-525-2508. www.schubas.com.
Schuba's has hosted live music from country to indie rock and

NIGHTLIFE

everything in between for two decades in its Baroque "Schlitz" corner bar and has recently expanded to book the nearby Lincoln Hall (*2424 N. Lincoln Ave., 773-525-2501*).

Comedy Clubs

ComedySportz
See p101. 929 W. Belmont Ave.

ImprovOlympic
3541 N. Clark St., Lakeview. 773-880-0199. www.improv olympic.com.
Primarily a club for aspiring comics, ImprovOlympic features an array of ensemble revues performed by teams of comedians-in-training. Shows run in two theaters seven days a week; some start as late as midnight.

Chemically Imbalanced Comedy
1422 W. Irving Park Road., Lakeview. 773-865-7731. www.cicomedy.com.
Chemically imbalanced showcases stand-up, improv, sketch comedy, plays, and short films and also offers improvisation classes.

The Second City
1616 N. Wells St., Old Town. 312-337-3992. www.secondcity.com.
What would we do without The Second City? Its satirical improv comedy has shaped the national sense of humor since the television show *Saturday Night Live* took to the air in 1975. The troupe was founded in Hyde Park in 1955 as the Compass Players. Scores of comedians started here, including Alan Alda, Elaine May, Ed Asner, Ann Meara, Joan Rivers, and a

The Second City

The Second City

galaxy of *SNL* stars led by John Belushi, Dan Aykroyd, Gilda Radner, and Mike Myers (the voice of Shrek). The hilarity continues with regular no-holds-barred revues nightly on the Mainstage, the E.T.C. stage, and Donny's Skybox.

Zanies
1548 N. Wells St., Old Town. Box office 312-337-4027. www.chicago.zanies.com. General admission charges start at $22, but prices vary. Minimum entry age is 21.
The oldest comedy club in the city (and now the country), this well-worn venue has been running for 30 years and has outlasted a dozen glitzier competitors. Name any stand-up comedian, and chances are he or she has performed here. The club usually features three comics a night: two up-and-coming performers and a well-known headliner. Zanies also has premises in Main, Nashville, St. Charles and Vernon Hills.

PERFORMING ARTS

Chicago's theater and performing-arts scene is extraordinarily diverse and accomplished. With over 120 professional theater companies, Chicago offers everything from popular Broadway musicals to gritty "off-Loop" productions. Traditional and contemporary ethnic dance troupes and opera and ballet companies make their home here, and music of all kinds flows nightly. Below are some suggestions for a night at the theater.

BOX OFFICE

Chicago Theater District

Many of the Loop's glorious 19C movie, vaudeville, and stage theaters are gone now, but a few have been preserved and renovated, and new venues have been added. The theaters below are located throughout the Loop, but tend to cluster in the area bounded by Washington Street, Lake Street, LaSalle Street, and Wabash Avenue. *Except where noted, you can purchase tickets for the Chicago Theater District venues online at: www.ticketmaster.com.*

Auditorium Theatre
50 E. Congress Pkwy. 312-922-2110. www.auditoriumtheatre.org.
The granddaddy of Chicago's historic theaters, this classic venue, which opened in 1889, makes for theater-going at its best. Its fine acoustics and lovely, renovated spaces are a delight. Programming varies from local dance troupes such as the Joffrey Ballet (see p121) to Broadway musicals.

Cadillac Palace Theatre
151 W. Monroe St. 312-986-5853. www.broadwayinchicago.com.
This lavish venue, inspired by historic French palaces, started out in 1926 as a vaudeville house. It later featured both movies and live stage shows. Renovated and reopened in 1999, the Cadillac

Palace now hosts pre-Broadway hits such as *The Producers* and other big-time musicals.

Chicago Theatre
175 N. State St. 312-462-6300. www.thechicagotheatre.com.
Opened as a movie palace in 1921, the glittering Chicago Theatre was resurrected, restored, and reopened in 1986. Frank Sinatra performed the opening concert, and today the schedule ranges from Bonnie Raitt to the National Acrobats of Taiwan.

©Chicago Theatre

Chicago Theatre

For up-to-the-minute information and links to Chicago theaters and performing-arts organizations, check out the website of the League of Chicago Theatres: *www.theatreinchicago.com*.

Gene Siskel Film Center
164 N. State St. 312-846-2600.
www.siskelfilmcenter.org.
Founded in 1972 by the School of the Art Institute, the GSFC is a major center of cinematic art and history. The state-of-the-art facility screens new American and foreign films, independent productions, and retrospectives.

Goodman Theatre
170 N. Dearborn St. 312-443-3800.
www.goodmantheatre.org.
Long located adjacent to the Art Institute, the formidable Goodman Theatre moved in 2000 to this newly constructed home in the Loop. The theater still features classic and contemporary works of serious drama on its two stages.

Goodman Theatre

© Jeff GoldbergESTO/Goodman Theatre

Oriental Theatre/Ford Center for the Performing Arts
151 W. Randolph St. 312-986-6863.
www.broadwayinchicago.com.
The "hasheesh-dream décor" of this 1926 theater that delighted silent-movie audiences has been restored for modern theater-goers. Large-scale stage productions such as *Ragtime, Fosse,* and *Mamma Mia!* make a splash here.

Bank of America Theatre/ Shubert Theatre
18 W. Monroe St. 312-986-6821.
www.broadwayinchicago.com.
The Shubert was built as the Majestic Theatre, a popular vaudeville venue, in 1906. Along with box-office hits such as *Cabaret* and *Rent,* it's now known for such pre-Broadway engagements as *Sweet Smell of Success* starring John Lithgow, and *Movin' Out,* a collaboration by Twyla Tharp and Billy Joel. In 2005 a $40 million renovation morphed the cramped quarters of The Shubert into a performance space with the décor of old, but with the amenities of the 21C.

Aragon Entertainment Center
1106 W. Lawrence Ave.
773-561-9500.
This 1926 ballroom was built to look like a Spanish village, and it still retains that European charm, all these decades later. In its heyday, names like Tommy Dorsey graced its stage. Today, nestled in the gentrifying Uptown neighborhood, the Aragon is not the crown jewel it once was, but still a gem. The venue hosts many live music concerts, various television progams, boxing and wrestling matches, and it can also be hired

MUST DO

for private functions.
Both English- and Spanish-
language stars play here.

Beverly Arts Center
2407 W. 111th St. 773-445-3838.
www.beverlyartcenter.org.
This South Side performance hall
has an intimate stage for music
concerts, dance, and plays.
The center is home to an annual
Irish Film Festival and other
cinematic events.

Music and Dance

Chicago Symphony Orchestra
220 S. Michigan Ave.
312-294-3333. www.cso.org.
Over the last 112 years, the CSO
has built a global reputation, which
continues under the baton of new
Music Director Riccardo Muti, who
arrived in 2010. During the season
(Sept–June), barely a night goes by
without music at the CSO's new
Symphony Center.

Hubbard Street Dance Chicago
Various venues around Chicago.
312-850-9744. www.hubbard
streetdance.org.
For sheer athleticism and
exuberance, the 21 dancers in
Hubbard Street's main company
can't be beat. With a repertoire
that blends ballet, jazz, modern,
and ethnic dance and music
into a seamless whole, these
performances are always fun.

Joffrey Ballet
Auditorium Theatre,
50 E. Congress Pkwy.
312-739-0120. www.joffrey.org.
The nation's premier ballet
company for half a century, the
Joffrey has thrived in its Chicago

Out of the Loop
The Loop isn't the only place
to see good theater. Other
worthwhile venues outside the
Loop include the 440-seat **Apollo
Theater** *(2540 N. Lincoln Ave.; 773-
935-6100; www.apollochicago.com)*,
offering lighter musicals and
stage works; and the
Athenaeum Theatre *(2936 N.
Southport Ave.; 773-935-6860;
www.athenaeumtheatre.com)*,
which stages dance, performance
groups, and theater schools from
around the city in its 1,000-seat
main stage.

home under the artistic direction
of Ashley Wheater and Executive
Director Christopher Conway.
This first-class dance company
continues to thrill audiences
year-round.

Joan W. and Irving B. Harris Theater for Music and Dance
205 E. Randolph St. 312-334-7777.
www.harristheaterchicago.org.
Opened in November 2003,
the Harris Theater provides a
much-needed home base for
Chicago's midsize music and dance
companies. The interior of this
underground (literally) theater in
Millennium Park may not be glitzy,
but the sightlines and acoustics in

Hot Tix
Try snagging half-price, same-
day show tickets at one of the
Hot Tix outlets *(www.hottix.org)*
around the city: 72 E. Randolph St.,
Loop; 163 E. Pearson St.,
Magnificent Mile; 9501 N. Skokie
Blvd., in Skokie; and at all Tower
Records stores.

PERFORMING ARTS

Joan W. and Irving B. Harris Theater for Music and Dance

the 1,500-seat space are excellent. There are other **Millennium Park**★★★ *(see p61)* performing-arts venues. Curling stainless-steel ribbons frame Frank Gehry's state-of-the-art **Jay Pritzker Pavilion**★★★, host to a variety of musical performances *(www.millenniumpark.org/events.htm; see p61).*

Lyric Opera

20 N. Wacker Dr. 312-332-2244. www.lyricopera.org.
Chicago's major opera company occupies the stately Civic Opera House, which opened in 1929. The lavish theater seats over 3,500, and each season includes a classic or debuting American work.

Muntu Dance Theatre

Various venues around Chicago. 773-241-6080. www.muntu.com.
Founded in 1972, Muntu (which means the "essence of humanity" in Bantu) performs contemporary and historic African, Caribbean, and African-American dance and music that pulse with rhythm and color.

Ruth Page Center for the Arts

1016 N. Dearborn, Gold Coast. 312-337-6543. www.ruthpage.org
This 1927 building houses a school of dance, studios, archives, and a 200-seat theater that showcases more than two dozen Illinois dance companies every year.

Chicago Theater Companies

Bailiwick Repertory Theatre

1229 W. Belmont Ave. 773-883-1090. www.bailiwick.org.
Anything goes here: From the raucous *Naked Boys Singing!* to Shaw's *St. Joan*, you'll find it all at this theater. The Bailiwick Arts Center boasts a 150-seat main stage, a 90-seat studio, and a 40-seat loft.

Chicago Shakespeare Theater

800 E. Grand Ave., on Navy Pier. 312-595-5600. www.chicago shakes.com.
Shakespeare would love the carnival atmosphere of Navy Pier, where this delightful 500-seat

Steppenwolf Theatre

© City of Chicago/GRC

Touring Tip

Planning to attend a performance at the Shakespeare Theater? Make dinner reservations at **Riva** *(700 E. Grand Ave.; 312-644-7482; www.stefanirestaurants.com/riva. htm)* for a delicious pre-show meal with great lake and city views.

courtyard theater stages marvelous interpretations of the Bard's works as well as other dramatic, comedic, and musical productions.

Steppenwolf Theatre
1650 N. Halsted St. 312-335-1650. www.steppenwolf.org.
You know their names: John Malkovich, Gary Sinise, William Peterson, Martha Plimpton, Joan Allen, John Mahoney, Laurie Metcalf, and so many others. They all did their early work at Steppenwolf, Chicago's premier off-Loop theater.
The 510-seat Downstairs Theatre, the largest of three, features world premieres and new interpretations of the classics with a focus on the ensemble acting that made Steppenwolf famous. Upstairs and in the Garage Theater, emerging artists and new plays rule.

Victory Gardens Theater
2243 N. Lincoln Ave. 773-871-3000. www.victorygardens.org.
Acclaimed for its productions of new and living playwrights, the VGT owns the historic Chicago Landmark building, the **Biograph Theater**. The VGT expanded it for use as a live venue and named it Victory Gardens at the Biograph. World premieres are a specialty at Victory Gardens Theater, so be the first on your block to see an exciting new work.

Ravinia Music Festival
200 Ravinia Park Rd., Highland Park. 847-266-5100. www.ravinia.org.
This world-famous outdoor festival spreads out over 36 lush acres in the North Shore suburb of Highland Park. Summer home of the Chicago Symphony Orchestra since 1936, Ravinia today offers everything from jazz, pop, and chamber music to folk, dance, and children's programs. The complex includes several restaurants, covered pavilion seating, and two indoor theaters. Most fun, though, is to enjoy summertime performances with a picnic dinner on the lawn—with or without candelabra.

PERFORMING ARTS

RESTAURANTS

The venues listed below were selected for their ambience, location, and/or value for money. Rates indicate the average cost of an appetizer, an entrée, and a dessert for one person (not including tax, gratuity, or beverages). Most restaurants are open daily (except where noted) and accept major credit cards. Call for information regarding reservations, dress code, and opening hours. For a list of restaurants organized by theme (Special Occasion, Easy on the Budget, etc.), *see p138.*

Luxury	**$$$$**	Over $50	*Inexpensive*	**$$**	$15–$30
Moderate	**$$$**	$30–$50	*Budget*	**$**	Under $15

Luxury

Arun's
$$$$　　**Thai**
4156 N. Kedzie Ave., Wrigleyville.
Dinner only. Closed Mon.
773-539-1909.
www.arunsthai.com.
Located in a nondescript neighborhood is Arun's, reputedly among the best Thai restaurants in the country. Arun's does not offer a standard menu, preferring to serve a 12-course—and popular—prix-fixe menu *($75 and up).*
Against a backdrop of mahogany, Thai silk, wall murals, and Thai craftwork, diners here can sample a delightful array of delicacies

Lad Nar, Arun's

and flavors selected and blended with exquisite attention to detail. Semi-private alcoves are perfect for couples and smaller parties. Whereas the six appetizer courses are served one by one, the entrées are served family style. Choices can range from snapper in red tamarind sauce to "golden baskets," a house specialty of shrimp-and-chicken-filled pastries. The meal ends with Arun's palate-cleansing lemongrass elixir. Arun's also has a fine wine list and full bar to complement your meal.

Charlie Trotter's
$$$$　　**New American**
816 W. Armitage Ave., Lincoln Park.
Dinner only. Closed Sun & Mon.
Jackets required. 773-248-6228.
www.charlietrotters.com.
Tables at the restaurant run by culinary genius Charlie Trotter get booked 4 to 12 weeks in advance. The draw? One-of-a-kind dishes prepared with naturally raised meats, organic produce, and vegetable-based sauces. Choose from two daily eight-course prix-fixe menus, the grand dégustation menu *($135),* and the lighter vegetable menu *($115).* For a special treat, reserve the sole kitchen table, where cooking becomes performance.

MUST EAT

Charlie Trotter's
©Battman/Charlie Trotter's

Everest

$$$$ **French**

440 S. LaSalle St., in One Financial Place, Loop. 312-663-8920. Dinner only. Closed Sun & Mon. www.everestrestaurant.com.

Named for its lofty perch on the 40th floor of the Chicago Stock Exchange, Everest commands a sweeping view of the city. Award-winning chef Jean Joho (also of Brasserie Jo; *p126*) crafts the finest seasonal ingredients into mouth-watering creations, adding accents from his native Alsace. Order à la carte to sample some of Joho's signature dishes—foie gras terrine, apple and Alsace Tokay gelée; roasted Maine lobster in Alsatian Gewurztraminer butter and ginger—or be adventurous and try the tasting menu *(seven courses for $89).*

L20

$$$$ **Seafood**

2300 N. Lincoln Park West. Lincoln Park. 773-868-0002. www.l2orestaurant.com.

Chef Laurent Gras gained fans in New York and San Francisco (not to mention France) before he moved to Chicago. His seafood-centric restaurant almost immediately had an obsessive following. Housed in the former Ambria space, L20 fuses Japanese and European influences for its fresh-from-the-sea approach. If you can't decide with all the good dishes on the menu, try one of two prix-fixe options: a four-course menu for $110 or a 12-course tasting for $165.

Spiaggia

$$$$ **Italian**

980 N. Michigan Ave., 2nd floor of One Magnificent Mile Building, Magnificent Mile. Dinner only. Jackets required. 312-280-2750. www.levyrestaurants.com.

Overlooking Oak Street Beach and Lake Michigan through its floor-to-ceiling windows on the north end of Michigan Avenue, Chicago's classiest Italian restaurant offers a soaring array of dishes that are well grounded in regional Italian cuisine. Pastas are handmade; meat and fish are wood-roasted—try the signature Colorado lamb chop with polenta and Brussels sprouts. Next door, dressed-down **Café Spiaggia** *(lunch Mon–Sat, dinner nightly, brunch Sun)* serves tasty pizzas and pastas at more palatable prices.

RESTAURANTS

125

Tru

$$$$ **New American**
*676 N. St. Clair St., Magnificent
Mile. Dinner only. Closed Sun.
Reservations required. 312-202-
0001. www.trurestaurant.com.*

At once lush and spare, the
dining room at Tru sets the
stage for the epicurean theater
to follow. Original Warhols and
other artworks add color to the
room, and the tables are serenely
minimalist. After you choose
from four prix-fixe menus, the fun
begins. Award-winning chefs Rick
Tramonto and Gale Gand (of Food
Network fame) send out course
after course, each more exquisite
than the last in both food and
presentation. These are not large
courses, mind you, but jewel-like
creations to tease the palate.
Dinner takes about three hours
when served this way, but it's a
lovely, sensual experience.

Moderate

Bistro 110

$$$ **French**
*110 E. Pearson St., Magnificent
Mile. 312-266-3110. www.bistro
110restaurant.com.*

The roasted garlic bulb that
accompanies your baguette at
this bright, bustling French bistro
sets the tone for the wood-oven-
roasted meats and fish served
here—all redolent with garlic.
Good basic *steak au poivre* and
steaks frites are sure to satisfy, as
are bistro favorites like cassoulet
Toulousian and Robuchon lamb
shank, slow-roasted in its own
juices. This is a great place for a
lunch break while shopping on
Mag Mile.

Blackbird

$$$ **New American**
*619 W. Randolph St., Near West
Side. Closed Sun. 312-715-0708.
www.blackbirdrestaurant.com.*

In contrast to its stark white
exterior and minimalist décor, this
tiny Market District hot spot serves
dishes that are a feast for the eyes,
prepared in a style that acclaimed
chef Paul Kahan describes as
"seasonal American with French
countryside influences." The name
Blackbird comes from French slang
for a plump Merlot grape. Try the
signature wood-grilled California
sturgeon, or perhaps a stuffed
breast of bobwhite quail with

Blackbird

©Blackbird

medjool dates, lobster mushrooms and white-corn grits. You never know what you might find; the menu and wine list both change frequently.

Blue 13
$$$ **New American**
416 W. Ontario St., River North. Dinner only. 312-787-1400. www.blue13chicago.com.
"Twisted American" is the theme of this rock-and-roll and tattoo-chic restaurant by Chris Curren and Man Marunowski that combines new American with French and Italian classics in a funky but decidedly upscale atmosphere. Subtle seafood dishes contrast with assertive meat preparation and a dizzingly delicious array of desserts.

🍴 Custom House Tavern
$$$ **Steakhouse**
500 S. Dearborn St. Printers Row. 312-523-0200. www.custom house.cc.
Certainly, Chicago has no shortage of steakhouses. But chef-owner Shawn McClain (Spring, Green Zebra) challenges the genre. Instead of oversized

Custom House Tavern

©Jeff Kauck/Custom House Tavern

portions of classics, he offers up new interpretations, using local ingredients and a minimalist aesthetic. Not for those who just want a slab of beef, but for those who are ready for a different side of the cow.

🍴 Green Zebra
$$$ **Vegetarian**
1460 W. Chicago Ave., River West. Dinner only. Closed Mon. 312-243-7100. www.green zebrachicago.com.
Chicago may be prized for its beef, but you couldn't tell it by Green Zebra, which has been packing in crowds of vegetarians since it opened in spring 2004. Named for a variety of heirloom tomato, this hot spot pulses with a hip vibe evident in its buzzing dining room and techno-modern décor. Chef Shawn McClain displays his culinary artistry using the freshest offerings of the season in selections like silky avocado panna cotta with tomato gelée, crème fraiche and sweet corn chips; and cave-aged-gruyère soufflé with endive and heirloom apples. Save room for the

Green Zebra

©Will Engelmann/Green Zebra

white-chocolate dreamsicle, with vanilla-bean ice cream, orange granité, and ginger soda.

Gilt Bar

$$$ **American**
230 W. Kinzie Ave., River North. 312-464-9544. www.giltbar chicago.com
This new spot behind the Merchandise Mart is great for a drink from the expansive cocktail menu as well as a comforting selection of pastas, seafood, and meat dishes by chef Brendan Sodikoff. Downstairs, the cash-only Curio bar offers two dozen hand-crafted cocktails in a speakeasy environment.

Harry Caray's

$$$ **American**
33 W. Kinzie Ave., River North. 773-465-9269. www.harrycarays.com.
Cubs fans will revel in the atmosphere here, which is chock-full of baseball memorabilia and items relating to the Hall of Fame career of late baseball announcer Harry Caray. House specialty chicken Vesuvio (chicken sautéed with garlic, then baked with crispy

potatoes and served with peas and a white-wine reduction) and 23-ounce Prime Porterhouse steaks top the menu. The 60-foot-long bar makes a great gathering place. Prices range widely so there's something for everyone.

The Publican

$$$ **New American**
837 W. Fulton Market, Near West Side. 312-715-0708. www.the publicanrestaurant.com.
This new beer-focused restaurant specializes in pork, shellfish, and sausage, paired with fine specialty ales and lagers. The space evokes a European beer hall with simple, sturdy lines that compare with the straightforward approach to food, stripped of adornment by Executive Chef Paul Kahan and Chef de Cuisine Brian Huston.

Rhapsody

$$$ **New American**
65 E. Adams St., Loop. Closed Sun. 312-786-9911. www.rhapsodychicago.com. No gym shoes, jeans, or shorts.
Much of the charm of this elegant urban dining spot derives from

The Publican

©Bob Briskey Photography/The Publican

Rhapsody

its location in Symphony Center at the heart of Chicago's Loop, which is framed beautifully in the restaurant's glass window-walls. Eclectic and inventive dishes (Coq au Vin blanc, Nantucket Bay scallops glazed with orange reduction) and desserts worthy of an encore draw on flavors from around the world. Wrap up your meal with the aptly named Chocolate Symphony, a sampling of bittersweet chocolate crème caramel, molten chocolate brownie, and white praline hot chocolate. Reserve early on performance nights.

Russian Tea Time
$$$ Russian
77 E. Adams St., Loop. 312-360-0000. www.russianteatime.com.
Distinguished by red-velvet furnishings, this elegant (if over the top) tea room located one block from the Art Institute buzzes with the polite chatter of classical-music lovers when the symphony performs. Fine caviar and champagne are de rigueur in the evening, as is tea in the afternoon. The restaurant also offers a complete menu for lunch and dinner featuring Russian, Uzbek, Ukrainian, and Baltic delicacies.

Like Rhapsody, this is another restaurant that's popular with the symphony crowd, so reserve early.

Saloon Steakhouse
$$$ American
200 E. Chestnut St., Magnificent Mile. No lunch weekends. 312-280-5454. www.saloonsteakhouse.com.
There are plenty of good steakhouses in Chicago. It's the atmosphere at the Saloon that sets it apart—more a neighborhood tavern than a swanky steakhouse. The room is small, but comfortable, and the steaks, vegetables, and potato sides keep 'em coming back for more. Among its other fine cuts, The Saloon serves Wagyu beef, which is American-raised Kobe-style beef. Added benefits: The service is friendly and the wine list is long.

Topolobampo
$$$ Mexican Regional
445 N. Clark St., River North. Closed Sun & Mon. 312-661-1434. www.fronterakitchens.com.
Chef Rick Bayless has given his sophisticated cuisine a nationwide reputation by the skillful blending of traditional Mexican flavors from Yucatan to Oaxaca. The

RESTAURANTS

chef's way with chilies and mole is particularly notable, and fish dishes excel. The menu changes every two weeks, but *puerco en manchamanteles* (Maple Creek Farm pork loin in red-chile sauce with plantains, pineapple and home-made chorizo) and *pescado en mole Amarillo* (pan-seared day-boat catch in Oaxacan yellow mole with smoked Prince Edward Island mussels and red-chile rice) are typical of the chef's culinary artistry. You'll find the same quality—at a lower cost—at the more casual **Frontera Grill**, which shares space with Topolobampo.

The Berghoff

©The Berghoff

Topolobampo

Topolobampo Restaurant

Inexpensive

17 West at the Berghoff
$$ **German**
17 W. Adams St., Loop.
Closed Sun. 312-427-3170.
www.17westchicago.com.
On the site of what was the 107-year-old beloved German restaurant called The Berghoff, 17 West blends contemporary bistro food with classic German fare. Look for modern takes on sauerbraten, schnitzel, and bratwurst. The

authentic 19C atmosphere, such as the carved wood bar, may make you want to linger.

Andies
$$ **Mediterranean**
5253 N. Clark St., Andersonville.
773-784-8616. www.andiesres.com.
It may be off the beaten path, but if you're shopping in Andersonville *(see p33)* at lunch or dinnertime, give Andies a try. A nice fireplace warms up the whitewashed room, which is clean and inviting. The menu blends Mediterranean and Middle Eastern flavors into an impressive montage of dishes at very reasonable prices. Ingredients are always fresh, and the service is friendly. Andies also features a kids' menu. You'll find another location a little farther south at 1467 W. Montrose Ave. *(773-348-0654)*.

avec
$$ **New American**
615 W. Randolph St.,
Near West Side. 312-377-2002.
www.avecrestaurant.com.
It is hard to believe that this small space was once intended to

handle the overflow from Blackbird. Instead, now avec, from the same crew that brings you Blackbird, is a destination in its own right. The communal tables are always packed, often with chefs from other restaurants. The strength of the menu is in its simplicity. The house-made charcuterie is legendary.

Note: avec does not accept reservations, so you are likely to wait for a table.

Café Ba-Ba-Reeba!
$$ **Spanish**
2024 N. Halsted St., Lincoln Park. 773-935-5000. www.leye.com.
Though other tapas bars have cropped up since, this was Chicago's original.
Seven seating areas decked in bright Mediterranean colors accommodate 360 diners. Ambience and food still sizzle, and the crowds come to enjoy hot and cold tapas ("little dishes" ordered in quantity and shared), paella, and a nice selection of Spanish wines.

Club Lucky
$$ **Italian**
1824 W. Wabansia Ave., Bucktown. 773-227-2300. www.club-lucky.com.
In a neighborhood where eateries come and go, Club Lucky has endured. Generous portions of homestyle Italian cooking—rigatoni with veal meatballs, eggplant parmigiana, shrimp scampi, chicken oreganato—great martinis and a funky 1940s supper-club atmosphere team up to make this lounge/restaurant a long-lived hit.

Erwin
$$ **American**
2925 N. Halsted St., Lakeview. Dinner only (brunch Sun). Closed Mon. 773-528-7200. www.erwincafe.com.
Seasonal specialties with Midwestern flavor grace Erwin's simple but robust menu. Creative vegetable and fruit preparations and savory sauces embellish basics like calves' liver, pan-roasted Great Lakes whitefish, wood-grilled pork chops, and even hamburgers—served with fries, horseradish

Shrimp Paella, Café Ba-Ba-Reeba!

RESTAURANTS

slaw, and home-made pickles. The smallish room is casual yet chic and comfortable, with the cozy feel of a friend's dining room.

Gino's East
$$ **Pizza**
633 N. Wells St., River North. 312-943-1124. www.featuredfoods.com.
Chicago's favorite deep-dish pizzeria, renowned for its two-inch-thick pies and its graffiti-splattered wooden booths, which have been moved to a new location in the space once occupied by Planet Hollywood. Call ahead and order your pizza, or be prepared to wait at least 30 minutes for your pie to cook.

Gino's East

©Gino's East

Heaven on Seven
$$ **Cajun**
111 N. Wabash Ave., 7th floor of Garland Building, Loop. Breakfast & lunch Mon–Sat. Dinner third Fri of month (reservations required). Closed Sun. 312-263-6443. www.heavenonseven.com.
Creole shrimp, crab cakes, po-boy sandwiches and gumbo are just a few of the New Orleans-style dishes served in this small but bustling lunchroom. Most entrées are served plenty spicy, but connoisseurs of Cajun heat use the bottles of Louisiana hot sauce on the tables to season their food. For a sweet ending, try a healthy serving of cinnamon-spiked bread pudding. A slicker version of the original, **Heaven on Seven on Rush**, is at 600 N. Michigan Ave., 2nd floor *(312-280-7774)*.

Revolution
$$ **Gastropub**
2323 N. Milwaukee Ave., Logan Square. 773-227-2739. www.revbrew.com.
When it opened in 2010, it was impossible to get a table at this no-reservations brewpub. The beers, pizza, and burgers became legendary and time has only added to the luster. Try the Iron Fist Pale Ale, or hop-lovers will enjoy the Anti-Hero IPA. Cognoscenti will savor the saison-style Coup d'Etat. Try the Farm Burger with spinach, horseradish, roasted beet, and a fried egg on top!

Budget

Ann Sather
$ **Swedish-American**
909 W. Belmont Ave., Lakeview. No dinner Mon, Tue. 773-348-2378. www.annsather.com.
A welcoming atmosphere and home cooking with a Swedish flair have made this a favorite among Chicagoans since 1945. Breakfast is a specialty—think Swedish pancakes with lingonberries, or Swedish meatballs. And be sure to try the home-made cinnamon rolls. Reasonably priced dinner entrées (baked chicken, Tom turkey, Lake Superior whitefish) come with two

sides and dessert. Belmont Avenue is the flagship, but Ann Sather also has other locations in Lakeview and Andersonville.

Chicago Pizza and Oven Grinder

The Chicago Pizza & Oven Grinder Restaurant

Chicago Pizza and Oven Grinder

$ Italian
2121 N. Clark St., Lincoln Park. Dinner only Mon–Fri, lunch weekends. 773-248-2570. www.chicago pizzaandovengrinder.com.
Located across the street from the site of the St. Valentine's Day Massacre, this nook in the basement of a Victorian brownstone serves unusual topsy-turvy pizzas that resemble potpies. Abundant salads can be shared and the grinders (the local term for submarine sandwiches) are generous. Good food and the laid-back atmosphere make this place popular and the waits sometimes long.

Ed Debevic's

$ American
640 N. Wells St., River North. 312-664-1707. www.featuredfoods.com.
"Good food, fresh service": that's the mantra of this Chicago institution, known for its sassy waitstaff who talk back and randomly jump up on the counter to sing. Kids and tourists seem to love it, and the diner fare—chili, burgers, hot dogs, meatloaf, ribs, milkshakes, and thick malts—isn't bad either.

Gold Coast Dogs

$ American
159 N. Wabash Ave., Loop. 312-917-1677.
The Chicago-style hot dog ranks with deep-dish pizza as a source of local culinary pride, and this busy stand serves up some of the best in town.
Though topping choices vary depending on individual taste, the Chicago-style dog (known as a "red hot") typically consists of a Vienna beef frank served on a poppy-seed bun. Mustard, relish, and onions are a must, and tomatoes, pickle slices, cucumber, lettuce, and both green and hot peppers are often added, along with a dash of celery salt. Ketchup, however, has no business on a red hot!

Green Door Tavern

$ American
678 N. Orleans St., River North. 312-664-5496.
Constructed only one year after the Chicago Fire of 1871, this is among the oldest downtown buildings and shows its age in a ten-degree list to the right and sloping floors. It's been a tavern since 1921 and today serves good burgers, sandwiches (try the triple-decker grilled cheese), and 35 different kinds of beer.

RESTAURANTS

Green Door Tavern

©Green Door Tavern

Hot Doug's
$ American
3324 N. California Ave,.
Logan Square. 773-279-9550.
The quintessential Chicago hot dog gets a gourmet makeover that has enthralled a vast loyal following over the last decade. Cognac-infused pheasant sausage with chive-Dijon goat's butter and duck rillettes? Or just a regular Chicago dog buried in a sea of vegetables, an affordable meal in an affable environment.

Half Shell
$ Seafood
676 W. Diversey Pkwy.,
Lincoln Park. 773-549-1773.
This quintessential neighborhood dive, dating to 1968, is located below street level; its downscale atmosphere is at odds with its surroundings, which have become quite upscale over the decades. Though small and dark, Half Shell lures loyal locals craving fresh crab legs, shrimp, oysters, and fried seafood for lunch or dinner. Diners are welcome to belly up to the curving bar, which takes up half the room, rather than wait for a table.

Lou Mitchell's
$ American
565 W. Jackson Blvd,.
Near West Side. 312-939-3111.
The place for breakfast (you can get lunch, too) in downtown Chicago since 1923, Lou Mitchell's still serves up manly portions of oatmeal, eggs, pancakes, French toast, and fluffy over-stuffed omelets to satisfy the heartiest appetites. Don't mind the plastic plants and the no-nonsense service. Or the Milk Duds.

Hema's Kitchen
$ Indian
2439 W. Devon Ave.,
West Rogers Park. 773-338-1627.
http://hemaskitchen.com.
Hema Potla and her family prepare awesome home-cooked Indian food in her little Far North Side restaurant. The wait can be awesome, too, especially on weekends, so be prepared. You can BYOB to enjoy while you wait. So popular has Hema's cooking become that she's opened another spot in Lincoln Park at 2411 N. Clark Street *(773-529-1705).*

Mr. Beef
$ Italian
666 N. Orleans St., River North.
Lunch only Mon–Sat. Closed Sun.
312-337-8500.
Tonight Show host Jay Leno put this place on the map. He discovered it as a struggling stand-up comic working the nightclub circuit and has been recommending it to his Hollywood pals for years. Go to Mr. Beef for the Italian beef sandwiches, consisting of a soft Italian roll piled high with thinly sliced marinated beef garnished with *giardinere* (pickled peppers, celery, and spices).

MUST EAT

The Third Coast

The Third Coast
$ **American**
*1260 N. Dearborn St.,
Gold Coast. 312-649-0730.
www.3rdcoastcafe.com.*
Sip cappuccino or claret in this
warm, comfortable coffeehouse
and wine bar, which is open early
and into the wee hours.
The clientele here ranges from
well-dressed Gold Coast matrons
to bohemian art students who stay
at the Three Arts Club across the
street. Good, light fare includes
soups, sandwiches, and salads. It's a
nice place to meet for lunch.

Twin Anchors
Restaurant-Tavern
$ **Barbecue**
*1655 N. Sedgwick St.,
Old Town. 312-266-1616.
www.twinanchorsribs.com.*
Beloved for its succulent, melt-in-
your-mouth ribs, Twin Anchors has
been a popular pub since it opened
after Prohibition; Frank Sinatra
stopped here regularly in the
1960s. The essential neighborhood
joint with its relaxed and modest
atmosphere makes a nice escape
from upscale chic.

Viet Bistro
$ **Vietnamese**
*1346 W. Devon Ave., Rogers Park.
773-465-5720.*
The family who was once behind
the beloved Pasteur opened this
more budget-friendly Vietnamese
eatery. While the menu may be
easier on the wallet than their
previous restaurant, the dishes
are still authentic. Pasteur fans are
happy to see the return of whole
red snapper on the menu. But Viet
Bistro is hipper than Pasteur ever
was, with fun tasting events and a
creative drinks menu.

Wishbone
$ **Southern**
*1001 W. Washington Blvd.,
Near West Side. No dinner Mon.
312-850-2663. www.wishbone
chicago.com.*
Have a heaping helping of hoppin'
John or mix and match down-
home side dishes with blackened
catfish and chicken étoufée.
The ultimate comfort food spot,
Wishbone's colorful, lively dining
room attracts an eclectic crowd,
from kids to celebrities, and serves
a hearty Cajun breakfast as well.
There's another location at 3300
N. Lincoln Avenue *(773-549-2663).*

RESTAURANTS

Wow Bao

$ **Asian**

835 N. Michigan Ave., in Water Tower Place, Magnificent Mile. 312-642-5888. www.wowbao.com.

If you want a quick bite while you're shopping on Mag Mile, Wow Bao serves up fresh steamed buns *(bao)* to business-lunchers and shoppers alike from their take-out booth just inside the Chicago Water Tower. Asian buns are served hot and stuffed with such combinations as Kung Pao chicken, spicy Mongolian beef, and green vegetables. Wash your selection down with ginger ale made with fresh ginger, or hibiscus iced tea. Rice bowls, salads, and soups are also available.

OAK PARK/EVANSTON

Maya del Sol

$$$ **Nuevo Latin**

144 S. Oak Park Ave., Oak Park. 708-358-9800.

Its not just the range of gourmet margaritas or the enticing green and red salsa that arrive with the chips. Maya brings the whole Mexican food experience to another level with exquisite, innovative but well-balanced dishes inspired by a range of South

Davis Street Fish Market

©Scott Shigley 2006/Davis Street Fish Market, Evanston

and Central American cuisines in addition to Mexico.

Campagnola

$$$ **Italian**

815 Chicago Ave., Evanston. 847-475-6100. www.campagnola restaurant.com.

With its emphasis on local and farm-fresh ingredients, a trip to Campagnola is like a little trip to Italy. The cozy space has tables pushed close together. You and your companions will dine on delicacies such as pork chops, pastas, and panna cotta. Rated one of the best Italian restaurants in Chicagoland, Campagnola focuses on locally sourced fresh ingredients. This is a great place for a date or a leisurely night out.

Chef's Station

$$ **American**

915 Davis St., Evanston. 847-570-9821. chefs-station.com.

Nestled under the train tracks in Evanston, Chef's Station is easy to walk by. But you shouldn't. It is surprisingly romantic, even with the train whizzing by, and the menu is simple, yet well done. The flash-fried spinach is translucent and unusual. Favorite entrées include the lamb, sole, and duck breast.

Davis Street Fishmarket

$$ **Seafood**

501 Davis St., Evanston. 847-869-3474. www.davisstreetfish market.com.

Forget those warnings you got about not ordering seafood in the Midwest. This unpretentious joint serves delicious, simply prepared fish and shellfish from the ocean, gulf, and Great Lakes. Decorated in

MUST EAT

a funky Key-West-meets-Nantucket style, the fishmarket forsakes haute cuisine for broiled, baked, sautéed, steamed, blackened, or fried fish, served with redskin potatoes and corn on the cob.

Tapas Barcelona
$$ **Spanish**
1615 Chicago Ave., Evanston.
847-866-9900. www.tapas
barcelona.com.
Colorful and noisy, Tapas Barcelona serves excellent "little plates," paellas, sandwiches, and even pizzas with an Iberian flare. Don't miss the *datiles con tocino*, a sinful concoction of baked fresh dates wrapped with bacon in a bell-pepper sauce. Reasonably priced Spanish wines are available by the glass or bottle, along with ports, sherries, and other cordials.

Union Pizzeria
$$ **Italian**
1245 Chicago Ave., Evanston.
847-475-2400. unionpizza.com.
Hip and the suburbs don't usually go together. But ever since this sleek pizzeria opened, city-dwellers have been hightailing to Evanston to see-and-be-seen and eat some of the area's best wood-fired pizzas. The restaurant also has an impressive beer and wine list. Union Pizzeria is owned by the folks who brought you Campagnola, and features the same focus on local fresh ingredients.

Dixie Kitchen
$ **Southern**
825 Church St., Evanston.
847-733-9030. www.dixiekitchen
evanston.com.
The music is loud and the crowd louder, but what else would you expect from a Cajun place? All the classics are on the menu here: fried green tomatoes, crawfish, jambalaya, black-eyed peas, and gumbo. The restaurant's breakfasts—served seven days a week—are popular with locals. Unlike many classic Southern eateries, Dixie Kitchen does have options for vegetarians.

Hemmingway's Bistro
$ **French**
211 N. Oak Park Ave., Oak Park.
708-524-0806. www.hemming
waysbistro.com.
Step back into the 1930s at this French bistro. Named for the author who was born in Oak Park (despite the misspelling), the eatery offers a seafood bar, plus French classics such as beef Wellington, coq au vin and duck a l'orange. The Sunday champagne brunch is popular.

Petersen's Ice Cream Parlor and Sweet Shoppe
$ **Ice Cream**
1100 Chicago Ave., Oak Park.
708-386-6131.
Since 1919, Petersen's has been a fixture in Oak Park. If you miss the old-time ice-cream parlor (and who doesn't?), stopping here is essential. Many a child (or disinterested spouse) has been convinced to go on walking tours of Frank Lloyd Wright homes with the promise of Petersen's afterwards. The hand-packed cones and quarts have an ice-cream density never found in the mass-market varieties! Don't skip the malt milkshake!

RESTAURANTS

137

RESTAURANTS BY THEME

Looking for the best restaurant for your special occasion? Want to see that star chef from the Food Network? In the preceding pages, we've organized the eateries by price category, so below we've broken them out by theme to help you plan your meals while you're in town. *Restaurants listed below are in Chicago unless otherwise noted.*

Breakfast Spots
Ann Sather *p132*
Lou Mitchell's *p134*
Wishbone *p135*

Easy on the Budget
Chicago Pizza and Oven Grinder *p132*
Ed Debevic's *p133*
Gold Coast Dogs *p133*
Green Door Tavern *p133*
Half Shell *p133*
Hema's Kitchen *p134*
Hot Doug's *p134*
Lou Mitchell's *p134*
Mr. Beef *p134*
The Third Coast *p135*
Wishbone *p135*
Wow Bao *p135*

Ethnic Experiences
Hema's Kitchen *p134*
Viet Bistro *p135*
Maya del Sol *p136*

Family Places
Andies *p130*
Ed Debevic's *p133*
Gino's East *p131*
Gold Coast Dogs *p133*
Petersen's Ice Cream *p137*

Hippest Décor
Blackbird *p126*
Green Zebra *p127*

Neighborhood Favorites
Bistro 110 *p126*
Maya del Sol (Oak Park) *p136*
Revolution *p132*

Chicago Pizza and Oven Grinder *p132*
Club Lucky *p131*
Erwin *p131*
Gino's East *p131*
Half Shell *p133*
Heaven on Seven *p132*

Pre-theater Dining
Rhapsody *p128*
Russian Tea Time *p128*

Restaurants with History
17 West at the Berghoff *p130*
Green Door Tavern *p133*

Special-Occasion Restaurants
Arun's *p124*
Charlie Trotter's *p124*
Everest (Jean Joho) *p124*
Spiaggia *p125*
Topolobampo *p129*
Tru *p125*

Small Plates (Tapas)
Café Ba-Ba-Reeba! *p130*
Tapas Barcelona (Evanston) *p136*

Star Chefs
Charlie Trotter's (Charlie Trotter) *p124*
Everest (Jean Joho) *p124*
Topolobampo (Rick Bayless) *p129*

Steakhouses
Custom House *p127*
Harry Caray's *127*
Saloon Steakhouse *p129*

HOTELS

The properties listed below were selected for their ambience, location, and/or value for money. Prices reflect the average cost for a standard double room for two people in high season. High season in Chicago is summer; rates are considerably less in low season. Price ranges quoted do not reflect the Chicago hotel tax of 15.4 percent. *For a list of hotels organized by theme (Posh Places, Hotels for Business, etc.), see p153.*

Luxury	**$$$$$**	Over $350	*Inexpensive*	**$$$**	$175–$250
Expensive	**$$$$**	$250–$350	*Budget*	**$$–$**	Under $175

Luxury

Four Seasons Hotel
$$$$$ **343 rooms**
120 E. Delaware Pl., Magnificent Mile. 312-280-8800 or 800-819-5053. www.fourseasons.com/chicagofs.
Done in lush fabrics, dark woods, and rich colors, guest rooms wrap visitors in luxury with marble baths and thick terry robes.
On the 32nd to 46th floors of the hotel, deluxe rooms afford sweeping views of Lake Michigan or the city skyline. For business travelers, "Executive-Tech" rooms feature additional data ports and a four-in-one fax machine/copier/scanner/printer. Work out in the large fitness facility, complete with an indoor pool. Once you've tired out those muscles, a trip to the hotel's urban spa might be in order. **Seasons Restaurant ($$$$)** serves contemporary American fare from local markets by chef Kevin Hickey in its opulent dining room; Chicagoans love it for Sunday brunch. Adjoining **Seasons Lounge** is a perfect place for afternoon tea with piano accompaniment.

The Peninsula Chicago
$$$$$ **339 rooms**
108 E. Superior St., Magnificent Mile. 312-337-2888 or 866-288-8889. www.chicago.peninsula.com.
A recent addition to Chicago's star-studded hotel lineup, the Peninsula (yes, as in the incomparable Hong Kong Peninsula) is indeed a luxurious stay. Quietly elegant, trim,

©Four Seasons/Peter Peirce

and classic, the hotel is nonetheless futuristic in its many appointments, which include steamless TV screens in the bathrooms. Spacious rooms, among the largest in the city, provide a minimum of 531 square feet, many with stunning views of the Magnificent Mile. The hotel's acclaimed health facilities boast a stunning pool and the 14,000-square-foot **Peninsula Spa**, which takes up the top two floors of the hotel. And **Avenues ($$$$)** restaurant consistently rates among the best in Chicago. Afternoon tea is served in the soaring lobby as live string music drifts down from a tiny balcony that overlooks the room. Royal Tea features chocolate buffet and fashion shows. The Shanghai Terrace serves Cantonese and Shanghainese delicacies while The Terrace offers light bites and exquisite cocktails.

Expensive

Amalfi Hotel
$$$$ 215 rooms
20 W. Kinzie St., River North.
312-395-9000 or 877-262-5341.
www.amalfihotelchicago.com.

At the Amalfi, your well-appointed room is your sanctuary, complete with Egyptian cotton linens, a pillow-top mattress and multihead shower. The concierge is your "Experience Designer"; he or she is available to consult with you upon arrival regarding all the hip things you want to do while you're in the neighborhood, and can be summoned throughout your visit to assist with crises or answer questions. While the hotel lacks a dining room, complimentary continental breakfast is served on each floor, and food can be ordered in from **Harry Caray's** restaurant *(see p127)* across the street. **Keefers ($$$)**, on the first floor, serves splendid steaks and chops.

The Drake Hotel
$$$$ 537 rooms
140 E. Walton Pl., Magnificent Mile.
312-787-2200 or 800-445-7667.
www.thedrakehotel.com.
Since 1920, the Italian Renaissance-style limestone building at the north end of the Magnificent Mile has been *the* address for visiting celebrities. Antique solid-brass candelabras and the original mahogany ceiling inset with hand-

The Drake Hotel

The Drake Hotel

The Fairmont Chicago

Fairmont Hotels and Resorts

painted tiles set the tone in the lobby. Rooms, some overlooking Lake Michigan, combine floral fabrics with dark woods. The old-fashioned (it opened in 1933) but respected **Cape Cod Room ($$$$)** serves—what else?—seafood at lunch and dinner in a business-casual atmosphere. The Drake is now a Hilton property. High Tea in the lovely Palm Court is a must while you're in Chicago *(see p30)*.

The Fairmont Chicago
$$$$ 692 rooms
200 N. Columbus Dr., Loop. 312-565-8000 or 800-866-5577. www.fairmont.com/chicago.
Rising just east of Millennium Park, the Fairmont has long provided a home away from home for political figures and celebrities. Spacious rooms are well appointed with soothing colors and contemporary style; you'll have your choice of city or lake views. Guests have access to the luxurious Lakeshore Athletic Club next door, with its six floors of workout facilities, including a 110-foot-high climbing wall and an eight-lane pool. And for business travelers, there's a full-service business center on-site. Tea is served each afternoon in the Lobby Lounge. This is a great location for attending summer music festivals.

InterContinental Chicago
$$$$ 807 rooms
505 N. Michigan Ave., Magnificent Mile. 312-944-4100 or 800 628-2112. www.interconti.com.
This Mag Mile classic began life as a men's club in 1929 and still retains many of the club's original decorative embellishments *(see p28)*. Egyptian, Renaissance, and Middle Eastern motifs ornament public spaces and ballrooms, giving the public areas a thoroughly exotic ambience, and lavish majolica tile sets off the hotel's celebrated junior Olympic-size swimming pool. South tower rooms are furnished in elegant Biedermeier style and have the best views; those in the north tower sport a more modern look. Dine on regional American dishes at **Zest ($$$)**, which has been remodeled with minimalist panache.

HOTELS

Lobby, James Chicago

©The James

James Chicago
$$$$ 297 rooms
55 E. Ontario St., Magnificent Mile.
312-337-1000 or 877-526-3755.
www.jameshotels.com.
Once the site of the family-friendly
Lenox Suites, the James Chicago
has quickly become the must-stay
locale for the young, hip, and
well-heeled. Swanky yet minimalist
rooms scream understated luxury,
while attentive service makes
everyone feel like a celebrity.
If you feel like a steakhouse
splurge, try the equally swanky
David Burke's Primehouse, on
the first floor. Burke is known for
having his own cattle, including
a stud named Prime.

The Raffaello Hotel
$$$$ 172 rooms
201 E. Delaware Pl., Magnificent
Mile. 312-235-6312. www.chicago
raffaello.com.
Rustic Old World charm emanates
from the beamed ceilings and
arched windows of this small hotel
located east of Michigan Avenue.
Less showy than other Michigan
Avenue boutique properties, the
the newly renovated Raffaello
claims to be the city's only luxury,
all no-smoking hotel.
Rooms are simple but spacious,
featuring one king or two
double beds.

Trump International Hotel and Tower
$$$$ 339 rooms
401 N. Wabash Ave.,
Magnificent Mile. 877-458-7867.
www.trumpchicagohotel.com.
The name says it all.
When Donald Trump puts his
last name on a hotel, you know
it is going to be expensive, but
also packed with amenities.
Rooms at the new Trump hotel
have floor-to-ceiling windows, so
you have excellent views of the
Chicago River and the skyline.

Trump International Hotel and Tower

Trump International Hotel and Tower

Guest room, Affinia Chicago

Affinia Chicago Hotel

The rooms have full kitchens, although it is hard to resist the hotel's restaurants.

W Chicago Lakeshore
$$$$ 556 rooms
644 N. Lakeshore Dr., Gold Coast. 312-943-9200 or 888-625-5144. Also at 172 W. Adams St., Loop. www.starwoodhotels.com.
Overlooking the lakefront, W's "spectacular" rooms afford great views of Navy Pier and the lake beyond, while those dubbed "wonderful" face the cityscape. With serenity in mind, the décor takes something of a Zen twist in its deep colors and strong lines. Rooms come equipped with electronic amenities including CD/DVD players, with a 24-hour CD library at your service.

Wheeler Mansion
$$$$ 11 rooms
2020 S. Calumet Ave., Near South Side. 312-945-2020. www.wheelermansion.com.
A stay here will give you a glimpse into life on Chicago's once-elegant Near South Side. Built in 1870, just a year before the Chicago Fire, this landmark is located in the **Prairie Avenue Historic District**★,

not far from Glessner House *(see p74)*. Individual room decorations suggest a 19C style, with dark wood trim, antique queen beds, and marble baths, all private. The house is conveniently located for South Side activities, including conventions at McCormick Place, and is not far from the lakefront. Complimentary gourmet breakfast and parking are included with your reservation.

Inexpensive

Affinia Chicago
$$$ 215 rooms
166 East Superior St., Magnificent Mile. 312-787-6000 or 800-367-7701. www.affinia.com.
Once the home of the Fitzpatrick Hotel, the Affinia Chicago brings another hip boutique hotel to the Mag Mile area. The luxury property includes a pillow menu, with six different options! The hotel's fish and chops restaurant, **C-House**, attracts lots of local buzz.

Allerton Hotel Chicago
$$$ 443 rooms
701 N. Michigan Ave., Magnificent Mile. 312-440-1500. www.theallertonhotel.com.

HOTELS

The Allerton has served Chicago as a hotel since 1924, and a renovation has nicely restored its original polish inside and out. Guest rooms are outfitted with marble baths and glow with warm wood tones and a rich palette of wall and fabric colors. Check out the view from the top-floor fitness center. The famous Tip-Top-Tap that once occupied the 23rd floor has been moved to the second floor and transformed into **Taps on Two ($$$)** French bistro.

Conrad Chicago
$$$ 311 rooms
521 N. Rush St., Magnificent Mile.
312-645-1500. www.conrad
hotels.com.
With Nordstrom—including Nordstrom Spa—and the entire North Bridge mall at your doorstep, the shopper staying at Conrad Chicago wants for nothing (you don't even need to go outside to reach the mall). Of course, the hotel is convenient to the entire Mag Mile, and its opulence is contemporary and understated with honey-tone woods, neutral colors, and clean lines.

Hard Rock Hotel
$$$ 381 rooms
230 N. Michigan Ave., Loop.
312-345-1000. www.hardrock
hotelchicago.com.
Smack-dab between the Loop and the Mag Mile, this newish property has convenience and a lot more going for it. The jazzy Art Deco Carbide and Carbon building has been skillfully converted to accommodate this cool new hotel. Integrating the best of the old with a bit of new dazzle, including a moderate number of rock 'n' roll artifacts, the Hard Rock manages a high degree of sophistication. Modern guest-room amenities include flat-screen TVs, DVD/CD 5-disc changers, free WiFi and dual-line phones. It's a convenient walk from here to the many attractions up and down Michigan Avenue, as well as east to the lakefront and along the river.

Hotel 71
$$$ 454 rooms
71 E. Wacker Dr., Loop.
312-346-7100. www.hotel71.com.
Billing itself as an "urban hotel adventure," 71 has given a tired

Conrad Chicago

©Conrad Chicago

Sax Chicago, chairman's suite, media lounge

 *Courtesy of Thompson Hotels*

1950s hotel an extreme makeover. Though the façade retains a dated look, the interior public spaces and rooms have bold, upbeat colors, animal prints and ultrasuede, and sleek furniture. Light sculptures add a chic touch. Rooms on the north side overlook the Chicago River.

Sax Chicago
$$$ 367 rooms
333 N. Dearborn St.,
River North. 312-245-0333.
www.hotelsaxchicago.com.
Forget English-manor style and French-country charm, the Sax Chicago aims to rock your world. Flamboyantly decorated throughout, the hotel makes a fitting partner for the exuberant **House of Blues** restaurant/nightclub next door *(see p114).* The rooms feature lots of high-tech perks.
Located along the Chicago River in landmark Marina City, the complex also includes a 36-lane bowling alley, boat charters, a health club, a wine bar, and an upscale steakhouse.

Hyatt Regency Chicago
$$$ 2,019 rooms
151 E. Wacker Dr., Loop.
312-565-1234. www.chicago
regency.hyatt.com.
If you're a Hyatt fan, welcome to the Mothership. This is the chain's largest property, and it's a behemoth. The glass-enclosed lobby, set about with greenery and fountains, can be something of an oasis, and the hotel's Big Bar sports the longest freestanding bar in North America, if such things matter. (As you might imagine, it

©Hyatt Regency Chicago

Hyatt Regency Chicago

HOTELS

145

serves everything BIG.) Its huge windows also offer good views looking north over the river. The hotel's location on East Wacker makes it convenient to destinations on both sides of the river, as well as Millennium Park and the lakefront. Chicago has several other Hyatt hotels as well.

Palmer House Hilton
$$$ 1,639 rooms
17 E. Monroe St., Loop.
312-726-7500 or 800-445-8667.
www.hiltonchicagosales.com.
Famous for its stunning hand-painted Beaux Arts ceiling, Empire Ballroom and lobby space, this Chicago fixture is dusting itself off with an interior renovation. The hotel's site on the corner of State Street in the Loop is convenient to shopping, dining, theater, Millennium Park, and the Art Institute, making it a favorite among conventioneers and visitors interested in downtown attractions. The Palmer House features **Trader Vic's Restaurant ($$$)**, something of a historic attraction itself for its oh-so-1950s Polynesian umbrella drinks.

Silversmith Crowne Plaza
$$$ 143 rooms
10 S. Wabash Ave., Loop.
312-372-7696 or 800-227-6963.
www.crowneplaza.com.
Tucked into Jeweler's Row just feet from the elevated tracks, the beautifully appointed Silversmith comes as an elegant surprise. Built in 1897 as a warren for jewelry makers, the National Historic Landmark was converted into a hotel and renovated in late 19C Arts and Crafts style. Rich oak paneling, glazed terra-cotta, and

Stickley furnishings throughout make a nice change from both hotel modern and B&B flounce. Don't be put off by the hotel's proximity to the elevated tracks; windows have been soundproofed. For extra quiet, however, ask for a room closer to the tenth floor.

Sofitel Chicago Water Tower
$$$ 415 rooms
20 E. Chestnut St., Magnificent Mile.
312-324-4000 or 800-763-4835.
www.sofitel.com.
The talk of all the architectural circles, the dramatic upside-down exterior and slick, too-cool interior of the new Sofitel live up to the buzz. The techno-hip lobby employs decorative lighting and artwork to distinct advantage, and the rooms carry through with sophisticated contemporary European styling.
Sofitel's sleek brasserie, **Café des Architectes ($$$)**, serves seafood and other dishes accented with Mediterranean, Asian, and Latin American flavors. Traditional French breakfasts in the Café are a must (unless you're counting calories!).

Swissôtel
$$$ 632 rooms
323 E. Wacker Dr., Loop.
312-565-0565 or 888-737-9477.
www.chicago.swissotel.com.
Designed by prominent Chicago architect Harry Weese, the Swissôtel cuts a crisp and shimmering 43-story silhouette, its triangular shape wrapped entirely in glass. The property exudes a quiet elegance, and the best thing about its spacious, well-appointed rooms (besides the doorbells) is the magnificent view from every

one. The Penthouse Health Club and Spa, one of the largest in a Chicago hotel, boasts all the necessities: lap pool, sauna, steam room, and whirlpool. Swissôtel caters largely to corporate travelers, so its business amenities—meeting spaces, a business center, secretarial services, and so on—are second to none. The hotel is undergoing a $64.5 million renovation, meaning the meeting space will be ready in June 2009 and a brand-new 54,000-square-foot ballroom will be completed toward the end of 2009.

Talbott Hotel
$$$ 147 rooms
20 E. Delaware Pl., Magnificent Mile. 312-944-4970 or 800-825-2688. www.talbotthotel.com.
Snug and intimate with an English fox-hunting theme, the classy Talbott features antiques and two fireplaces in its wood-paneled Victorian lobby. Guest rooms and suites, some with full kitchens, are simply but tastefully appointed in period reproductions. The hotel's overall tranquility transports guests far from the bustle of nearby Michigan Avenue, and the concierge can help with anything from procuring theater tickets to setting up a meeting. Guests here also enjoy nightly turndown service and complimentary access to the 72,000-square-foot Gold Coast Multiplex fitness facility.

The Whitehall Hotel
$$$ 221 rooms
105 E. Delaware Pl., Magnificent Mile. 312-944-6300 or 800 948-4255. www.thewhitehallhotel.com.
Just steps off the north end of Mag Mile (one block south of

haute-couture shopping on Oak Street; see p103), this venerable inn is among the original small hotels in the city, serving an elite clientele since 1974. Today it retains its polish thanks to a renovation that has refreshed its English country-manor atmosphere. Light-filled rooms are done in neutral tones offset by dark period furnishings. The attentive staff provides personalized service, and small pets (under 30 pounds) are accepted.

Budget

Best Western Hawthorne Terrace
$$ 59 rooms
3434 N. Broadway, Lakeview. 773-244-3434 or 888-860-3400. www.hawthorneterrace.com.
Nestled in a neighborhood on Chicago's North Side, the Hawthorne Terrace offers a charming boutique ambience convenient to Wrigley Field and the lakefront. Rooms have a vintage feel, with flowered wallpaper and bedspreads; many come equipped with whirlpool tubs, refrigerators and microwaves, and garden views. Enjoy a complimentary continental breakfast with your newspaper each morning. There's even a small workout room.

City Suites Hotel
$$ 45 rooms
933 W. Belmont Ave., Lakeview. 773-404-3400 or 800-248-9108. www.cityinns.com.
City Suites inhabits a neighborhood that bustles with street life day and night, crowded as it is with restaurants, bars, nightclubs, and even a tattoo parlor.

Queen deluxe room, Hotel Allegro

David Phelps/Kimpton Group

Most of the units in this Art Deco restoration are suites furnished with hide-a-beds and refrigerators, though some standard queen rooms are available for less. Unexpected amenities such as refrigerators, shaving/make-up mirrors, and robes make City Suites a good bet for the price. The elevated train just west provides rapid transportation to downtown.

The Essex Inn
$$ 267 rooms
800 S. Michigan Ave., Grant Park.
312-939-2800 or 800-621-6909.
www.essexinn.com.
Though its rooms are basic, the Essex appeals for its good prices and convenient location along South Michigan Avenue. A recent renovation added a garden pool and fitness center on the fourth-floor rooftop. Across the street, Grant Park makes a lovely front yard, and the hotel is within walking distance of the Loop, Millennium Park, the lakefront, and Art Institute.

Hotel Allegro Chicago
$$ 483 rooms
171 W. Randolph St., Loop.
312-236-0123 or 800-643-1500.
www.allegrochicago.com.
Bold colors and prints have transformed the North Loop theater district's 1926 Bismarck Hotel into a stylish Hollywood set. The lobby's fluted glass and oak-paneled walls are the backdrop for cobalt-blue velvet chaise longues and red velour sofas. Guest rooms sport contemporary colors (pumpkin-colored walls and oversize upholstered brown and cream headboards) and modern amenities (a sound system, a flat-screen TV, and WiFi). Traveling with your pet? Dogs and cats are welcome at Hotel Allegro, which even offers special packages for pets and their humans.

Hotel Burnham
$$ 122 rooms
1 W. Washington St., Loop.
312-782-1111 or 877-294-9712.
www.burnhamhotel.com.
Designed by Daniel Burnham's architectural firm in 1895, the

historic **Reliance Building★★** was restored in 1999 as the fanciful Hotel Burnham. Here original design elements, such as the mosaic floor and ornamental metal elevator grilles, blend with bold interior stylings, including royal-blue velvet headboards and matching cornices in the guest rooms. Conveniently located for shoppers, across from Marshall Field, the Burnham is also within walking distance of theaters, the Art Institute, Millennium Park, and the lakefront. Enjoy American comfort food in the hotel's **Atwood Café ($$$)**.

Hotel Monaco
$$ **192 rooms**
225 N. Wabash Ave., Loop.
312-960-8500 or 866-610-0081.
www.monaco-chicago.com.
Two blocks from the Loop or the Mag Mile, this boutique property was designed as the world traveler's 1930s Art Deco-style living room. In the oversize lobby, the registration desk is modeled after a classic steamer trunk. Guest rooms are done in dark woods and pistachio green in the French Deco

style. Whimsical amenities include an in-room pet goldfish on request and "tall" rooms with nine-foot beds and extra-high showerheads. If you're traveling with your entourage, check out the Rock Star Suite; it has hosted the likes of James Taylor and Britney Spears. In a bit of a contrast, down-home all-American cooking—including a red-wine-glazed meatloaf "TV dinner"—is available next door at **South Water Kitchen ($$)**.

Majestic Hotel
$$ **53 rooms**
528 Brompton Ave., Lakeview.
773-404-3499 or 800-727-5108.
www.majestic-chicago.com.
Going to a Cubs game? Located steps from Wrigley Field, as well as Lincoln Park and Belmont Harbor, this comfortable English-style inn is nicely situated for North Side activities. Of the 53 units, 22 are suites that include refrigerators, microwaves, and wet bars. Amenities include robes, morning newspaper, and a continental breakfast served in the lobby each morning. Prices dip considerably in the low season.

Hotel Burnham in the Reliance Building

Kimpton Group

HOTELS

Millennium Knickerbocker Hotel

$$ **305 rooms**

163 E. Walton Pl., Magnificent Mile.
312-751-8100 or 866-266-8086.
www.millenniumhotels.com.

Transformed several times since its construction in 1927, the Knickerbocker underwent a hugely expensive, relatively recent renovation. Its distinctive cathedral-style windows and lit marquee welcome guests as they did in Prohibition-era Chicago, and the breathtaking, 5,000-square-foot Crystal Ballroom (now used for meetings and special events) still echoes with the sounds of the Jazz Age. Rooms are small but comfortable. The **Martini Bar** serves 44 varieties of its namesake against a musical backdrop of live jazz piano.

Seneca Hotel

$$ **160 rooms**

200 E. Chestnut St., Magnificent Mile. 312-787-8900 or 800-800-6261. www.senecahotel.com.

Set in the shadow of the John Hancock Center, the venerable Seneca is a sturdy old residence hotel that offers travelers 160 rooms and suites with complete kitchens (including dishwashers) and comfortable rooms (100 additional rooms are reserved for residential guests). A stay here is a little like visiting grandmother, in all the good ways: nothing too fancy, but homey, sensible, and well situated. Just a block east of Michigan Avenue, the Seneca is within walking distance of the Museum of Contemporary Art and all the shops of Water Tower Place, the Mag Mile, and Oak Street. While it offers no dining facilities of its own, a deli, wine bar, and the **Saloon Steakhouse** *(see p129)* are located in the building, along with a full-service salon and spa.

Sutton Place Hotel

$$ **246 rooms**

21 E. Bellevue Pl., Magnificent Mile. 312-266-2100 or 866-378-8866. www.suttonplace.com.

Stylish and elegant, the modern 23-story Sutton Place caters to both business and getaway travelers. Comfortable rooms are custom furnished with contemporary flair and a hint of Art Deco design;

The Tremont Hotel

Starwood Hotels and Resorts

suites offer large living areas and wet bars. The marble baths are particularly nice here, with separate soaking tubs and showers. A full-service business center on the fourth floor offers everything from video-conferencing to document processing, and the sleek **Whiskey Bar** lounge is a perfect place to entertain clients.

The Tremont Hotel
$$ **130 rooms**
100 E. Chestnut St. Magnificent Mile. 312-751-1900 or 800-621-8133. www.tremontchicago.com.
Another lodging in the English style, the Tremont is named for a "luxury" hotel that opened in 1838. Its cozy lobby, complete with a fireplace, welcomes guests with manor-house ambience; likewise the bright rooms and suites. The Tremont House next door offers 12 furnished suites with kitchens for those traveling with families or desiring a longer stay. Named for the infamous former coach of "Da Bears," **Mike Ditka's ($$$)** restaurant is located in the hotel, with downstairs dining (think steaks and chops) and a cigar bar on the second level.

The Willows Hotel
$$ **55 rooms**
555 W. Surf St., Lincoln Park. 773-528-8400 or 800-727-3108. www.willowshotelchicago.com.
The Willows occupies a vintage 1920s building just off busy Broadway. Renovated in 19C French country style, the lobby is pretty in tones of pink and peach. Though bathrooms are small, the rooms are restful, done in a soft pastel palette. Not far away are Diversey Harbor, the Notebaert Nature Museum

The Willows Hotel
©Broughton Hotels

and Lincoln Park Zoo, along with shopping and dining on Broadway and surrounding blocks. Ask about the seasonal package deals.

Red Roof Inn
$ **208 rooms**
162 E. Ontario St., Magnificent Mile. 312-787-3580 or 800-733-7663. www.redroof.com.
Who'd have guessed it? A reasonably priced, perfectly suitable hotel just off the Mag Mile in one of Chicago's hottest neighborhoods? Even if the room does remind you of your last road trip, your checkbook will be ahead of the game.

STAYING IN OAK PARK AND EVANSTON

The Carleton of Oak Park Hotel and Motor Inn
$$ **154 rooms**
1110 Pleasant St., Oak Park. 708-848-5000 or 888-227-5386. www.carletonhotel.com.
Opened in 1928 as Oak Park's "high-class hotel," the Carleton offers pleasant accommodations convenient to downtown Oak Park and about 20 minutes from the Loop via the nearby elevated

HOTELS

The Carleton of Oak Park Hotel

train. Motor-inn rooms are slightly cheaper. Most rooms have microwaves and refrigerators.

The Homestead
$$ 90 rooms
1625 Hinman Ave., Evanston. 847-475-3300. www.thehomestead.net.
This colonial-style manse was built in 1928 as a genteel hotel "in a wonderful location." It still caters to both overnighters and extended-stay guests with single rooms, studios, and one- and two-bedroom apartments. Reservations include a continental breakfast and garage parking, and the rooms are simple but comfortable. The lakefront, downtown Evanston and the Northwestern University campus are all within walking distance, as are plenty of good places to eat.

Hotel Orrington
$$ 269 rooms
1710 Orrington Ave., Evanston. 847-866-8700 or 888-677-4648. www.hotelorrington.com.
After a $32 million renovation, the Orrington retains its lovely 1923 feel, while sporting a fresh interior design and added amenities.

All of its rooms, suites, banquet facilities, and common areas have been refurbished to please both vacation and business travelers and to attract meetings and gatherings. Located adjacent to Northwestern University and around the corner from Evanston's shopping and dining district, the Orrington is well placed for Evanston visitors.

The Write Inn
$ 111 rooms
211 N. Oak Park Ave., Oak Park. 708-383-4800. www.writeinn.com.
This suburban inn is located along a shady stretch of residential street just steps from Oak Park's historic attractions and trains to the Loop. It sits across the street from the Hemingway Museum, and just north you'll find Hemingway's Birthplace. Decorated with 1920s period antiques, rooms range from small chambers outfitted with Murphy beds to larger rooms featuring sitting areas, whirlpool tubs, and kitchenettes.

HOTELS BY THEME

Looking for good business hotels in Chicago? Want to bring Fido along? In the preceding pages, we've organized the properties by price category, so below we've broken them out by theme to help you plan your trip.
Hotels listed below are located in Chicago unless otherwise noted.

Close to Wrigley Field
Best Western Hawthorne Terrace *p147*
Majestic Hotel *p149*

Easy on the Budget
The Carleton of Oak Park Hotel and Motor Inn (Oak Park) *p151*
The Essex Inn *p147*
Red Roof Inn *p151*
The Write Inn (Oak Park) *p152*

For Business Travelers
The Fairmont Chicago *p140*
Four Seasons *p139*
Hard Rock Hotel *p143*
Hyatt Regency Chicago *p144*
Palmer House Hilton *p145*
Sofitel Chicago Water Tower *p145*
Swissôtel *p146*
Sutton Place Hotel *p150*

For Families
James Chicago *p141*
City Suites Hotel *p147*
Seneca Hotel *p149*
The Tremont Hotel *p150*
Wooded Isle Suites *p151*

Hippest Décor
Hard Rock Hotel *p143*
Hotel Allegro Chicago *p147*
Hotel Monaco *p148*
Hotel 71 *p144*
Sofitel Chicago Water Tower *p145*

Hotels with History
The Drake Hotel *p140*
The Homestead (Evanston) *p152*
Hotel Burnham *p148*
Hotel Orrington *p152*
InterContinental Chicago *p141*

Palmer House Hilton *p145*
Silversmith Crowne Plaza *p145*
Wheeler Mansion *p142*
The Willows Hotel *p151*

Near Mag Mile Shopping
Allerton Hotel Chicago *p143*
James Chicago *p141*
The Drake Hotel *p140*
Four Seasons Hotel *p139*
InterContinental Chicago *p141*
The Peninsula Chicago *p139*
Red Roof Inn *p151*
Seneca Hotel *p149*
Sofitel Chicago Water Tower *p145*
Sutton Place Hotel *p150*
Talbott Hotel *p146*
The Tremont Hotel *p150*
The Whitehall Hotel *p146*

Pet-Friendly Hotels
Hotel Allegro Chicago *p147*
Hotel Monaco *p148*
Sofitel Chicago Water Tower *p146*
W Chicago Lakeshore *p142*

Posh Places
Amalfi Hotel *p140*
The Drake Hotel *p140*
The Fairmont Chicago *p140*
Four Seasons Hotel *p139*
InterContinental Chicago *p141*
The Peninsula Chicago *p139*

Spa Experiences
The Fairmont Chicago *p140*
Four Seasons Hotel *p139*
The Peninsula Chicago *p139*
Swissôtel *p146*

HOTELS

153

CHICAGO

The following abbreviations may appear in this Index: NHS National Historic Site; **NM** National Monument; **NMem** National Memorial; **NP** National Park; **NHP** National Historical Park; **NRA** National Recreational Area; **NWR** National Wildlife Refuge; **SP** State Park; **SHP** State Historical Park; **SHS** State Historic Site.

INDEX

INDEX

Photo Credits (page icons)
Must Know
©Blackred/iStockphoto.com Star Attractions: 6–9
©Nigel Carse/iStockphoto.com Calendar of
Events: 10–11
©Richard Cano/iStockphoto.com Practical
Information: 12–19
Must Sees
©Tjrubin/Dreamstime.com Neighborhoods: 22–37
©Christophe Rarndt/iStockphoto.com Landmarks:
38–43
©Terraxplorer/iStockphoto.com Museums: 44–60
©Scott Cramer/iStockphoto.com Parks: 61–69
©Steve Geer/iStockphoto.com Historic Sites: 70–77
©Kutt Niinepuu/Dreamstime.com Excursions: 78–86

Must Dos
©Thomas Barrat/Fotolia.com Fun: 87–90
© Witold Skrypczak/Alamy Outdoor Fun: 91–92
©ALEAIMAGE/iStockphoto.com Kids: 93–101
©narvikk/iStockphoto.com Shop: 102–109
© Subbotina Anna/Fotolia.com Spas: 110–112
©Jill Chen/iStockphoto.com Nightlife: 113–118
©Shannon Workman/Bigstockphoto.com
Performing Arts: 119–123
©Marie-France Bélanger/iStockphoto.com
Restaurants: 124–138
©Larry Roberg/iStockphoto.com Hotels: 139–153

INDEX